MY HOME IS IN THE SMOKY MOUNTAINS

By

Herbert L. Hyde

Herbert L. Hyde

WORLDCOMM®
a division of Creativity, Inc.

Publisher: Ralph Roberts
Vice-President: Pat Roberts

Editors: Barbara Blood, Gayle Graham, Susan Parker

Cover Design: **WorldComm®**
Interior Design & Electronic Page Assembly: **WorldComm®**
Cover painting: T.J. Shytle
Interior painting: William Garrett Hyde

10 9 8 7 6 5 4 3 2

Library of Congress Catalog Card Number: 98-60860

ISBN 1-56664-133-0

WorldComm®—a division of Creativity, Inc.—is a full–service publisher located at 65 Macedonia Road, Alexander NC 2870. Phone (828) 252–9515, Fax (828) 255–8719.

WorldComm® is distributed to the trade by Alexander Books™, 65 Macedonia Road, Alexander NC 2870. Phone (828) 252–9515, Fax (828) 255–8719. For orders only: 1-800-472-0438. Visa and MasterCard accepted.

This book is also available on the internet in the **Publishers CyberMall™**. Set your browser to http://www.abooks.com and enjoy the many fine values available there.

CONTENTS

About the Author

Herbert Hyde was born and raised in the Great Smoky Mountains in Swain County, North Carolina. He has become widely known as a Man of The Mountains and a Man Of The State.

He is an Attorney at Law, located in Asheville, North Carolina and has been practicing as a trial lawyer since 1954.

During that time he served in the North Carolina Senate and the North Carolina House of Representatives, where he was known as the Last of the Great Orators. The Reading Clerk of the House of Representatives, upon retiring after thirty years of service there, cited him as the best speaker he had heard during those thirty years.

He also served as a member of the North Carolina Courts Commission, as Chairman of the State Commission For The Blind, and Secretary of the Department of Crime Control and Public Safety.

A graduate of Western Carolina University, which he was able to attend under the G. I. Bill, he was a Root-Tilden Scholar at New York University School of Law, where he earned his J.D. Degree in 1954.

He is a longtime member of the Bar of the United States Supreme Court and local Federal and State Courts and is a member of the North Carolina State Bar, the State Bar Association and the American Bar Association. He is a Fellow of the American College of Trial Lawyers.

A veteran of World War II, he served in Naval Intelligence in the Pacific Theatre.

He is married to the former Kathryn Long of Macon County, North Carolina and they are proud to have six children and five grandchildren.

Not only is he known as an orator, he is also known as a great story teller.

In this book are some of those stories from his boyhood in the Great Smoky Mountains of Swain County.

1

To Begin With

The best rule for any person to follow was never better stated than by Shakespeare's character, Polonius, in The Tragedy of Hamlet, Prince of Denmark, Act I, Scene iii, Lines 78-80.

"... to thine own self be true,
And it must follow, as the night the day,
Thou canst not then be false to any man."

After I grew up, I spent years in politics and I spoke often of my place of birth in the Smoky Mountains of Swain County in a one-room cabin. I even claimed—humorously, of course—that I was born in a log cabin which I built myself.

But I didn't advertise the name of the spot where I was born. It just wouldn't do for a politician to do that.

The place where I was born is called Windy Gap.

I was born there in the month of December during a terrible blizzard.

My Gram Ma Medlin—my mother's mother—was there to help her daughter through her second child birth. The first birth was of my brother Walt, almost two years older than I.

Gram Ma Medlin later told me that it was one of the coldest nights she had ever seen. The snow came in heavy and the drifts were over five feet deep. The temperature dropped way below zero and the cold wind blew hard through Windy Gap.

There was a fire place in that one-room cabin and also a wood-burning cook stove. Gram Ma Medlin said that Dad worked hard all night to keep the fires going in the fire place and in the cook stove.

Even so, she said, I almost froze to death. She was really worried about me.

And she said that there were holes in that cabin big enough to throw a dog out.

I let time go by and, after years, Gram Ma Medlin died and I never even thought to ask her how big a dog she was talking about.

Now, I will never know.

The place where I was born is located within an old grant of land from the State of North Carolina to Matthew Garrett, my Great, Great, Great Grandfather.

Scotch-Irish he was and he and his two brothers came over from Ireland to Charleston, South Carolina. There he met his bride. They were married and then, with her and his two brothers, he migrated to the Great Smoky Mountains.

The two brothers settled down in what became Haywood County but my Gram Pa Garrett went on west to an area that later became Swain County. There he settled down while the whole area was still Cherokee Indian territory.

Then, in 1819, the Cherokee Indians entered into a treaty by which they gave up all their lands east of the Tennessee River.

Then Gram Pa Garrett obtained a grant from the State of North Carolina for 640 acres of land, a square mile.

I was born on land within that grant.

Gram Pa Matthew Garrett had a son named William Garrett. He married Jane Hyatt Garrett. She was living when I was born and as I grew up she told me stories and sang me songs which I still remember.

She had three daughters: my Great Gram Ma Sarah Jane Garrett Penland, Aunt Lura (Lurie) Garrett Ball and Aunt Eliza (Lizie) Garrett Weeks. She also had some sons who kept the name Garrett going.

Aunt Lurie Ball and Aunt Lizie Weeks both lived on a part of the land for which Gram Pa Garrett got a grant. Aunt Lurie Ball was married to Will Ball and Aunt Lizie Weeks was married to Guge Weeks.

The place of my birth was east and over a small ridge from the head of Mountain Branch which flows into the Tuckaseigee River.

But I do not remember living in that cabin where I was born.

My first memory of a home was in Emma Field, about a mile north of the place of my birth, on a branch which flows into Lands Creek, which, in turn, flows into the Tuckasegiee River, west of Mountain Branch.

In Emma Field there were then located three houses. The house last downstream was the first home I remember. It was built by my Dad. It was made of plain planks and was without ceiling or insulation. It had a porch on the lower side and the porch and main part of the house set on stilts, made out of cut off logs setting on flat rocks. Above that part of the house was the kitchen and living room together with the fire place and chimney on the upper end of that room and a sloping yard running along and parallel with that room to the lower part of the house. The yard was plain dirt, without grass. We swept it with a broom.

Across a small ridge and downstream along the main branch which flowed past that house was a spring where we obtained our drinking water.

Also located on our place was a cow barn, a corn crib, a can house, a garden, a potato patch, a corn field, a pasture. And there were acres of woods where we obtained our fire wood and wood for the cook stove.

The middle house in Emma Field was the home of my maternal grand parents, Gram Pa Charles (Charlie) Lewis Medlin and Gram Ma Elizabeth (Lizzie) Buchanan Medlin, and their youngest daughter, Aunt Annie Medlin.

Upstream from that house was the home of my mother's brother, Uncle Charles Medlin, and his wife, Aunt Martha Gouge Medlin, and their children. Later that house was occupied by other families.

While we were still living in the lower house, my Aunt Annie Medlin married my Uncle Ottis Franklin. They later had a daughter and a son.

My Aunt Martha Gouge Medlin was visited often by her mother, whom we called Granny Gouge. She lived with her husband, John Gouge, over in Graham County in a village named Tuskeegee.

They had moved from Mitchell County to Swain County and then to Graham County.

Granny Gouge would visit her daughter for a week at a time but would spend each night at our house because there was more room there. That was after Gram Pa and Gram Ma Medlin moved out of the middle house and we moved into it. They moved to a house located less than a hundred feet from the spot where I was born.

When Granny Gouge spent those nights at our house, mostly in the winter time, we sat around the fireplace at night and she told us wonderful ghost stories, many of which scared me half to death. And she sang to us old ballads, most of which I still remember.

One of the clearest and fondest memories I have of Granny Gouge is that she never carried a suit case. She would come to spend a week and she would wear seven dresses, one over the other, over the other. She would come to our house and take off six dresses and leave them in our house. Then she would have a fresh dress for each day she stayed there. I never commented on that matter in front of her but I did sometimes refer to it as Snow White and the seven drawers.

After we moved to the middle house in Emma Field, Uncle John Frazier and his wife, Dora Medlin Frazier—my mother's oldest sister —moved into the lower house with their children.

When Gram Pa and Gram Ma Medlin moved to the house near the spot where I was born, they were living very close to the home of their son, Jud Medlin and his wife, Trula Bebber Medlin, and their children.

Uncle Jud Medlin was a Baptist preacher. He met his wife while Gram Pa and Gram Ma Medlin, and family, were living near Afton, Tennessee. Aunt Dora Medlin Frazier met her husband, John Frazier, there also.

Before that, Gram Pa and Gram Ma Medlin had moved to Texas, taken out a homestead and lived there a few years. They had moved there in 1888 but the depression of 1892 persuaded them to come back home. Later they lived a while in Tennessee. Then they came back to the land of their birth, on Hazel Creek in Swain County, all now a part of the Great Smoky Mountains National Park.

Gram Pa Medlin's father, Marion Medlin, had a village named for him on Hazel Creek. He was known as the Good Shepherd of the Hills. He ran a general store and was the postmaster of the village of Medlin, North Carolina. He also served as the local doctor, Justice of The Peace and Baptist minister.

There both Gram Pa Medlin and Gram Ma Medlin went to school and became literate.

The brother of Gram Ma Medlin, my Great Uncle Thomas Buchanan, was the first native of Swain County to graduate from any college.

On the other hand, Gram Pa Hyde and Gram Ma Hyde were both illiterate until Gram Ma Hyde had raised her nine children. Then she taught herself to read and write and eventually became an herb doctor, much renowned in her community.

In that she was following in the footsteps of her grandfather, William Garrett.

Gram Pa Hyde never learned to read or write but Gram Ma Hyde would read to him from the Bible and he would memorize seven or eight chapters at one time.

Gram Pa Hyde had two brothers: Uncle Mike Hyde and Uncle Fide Hyde.

They all lived in Swain County when I knew them. It was long after I grew up before I learned that all three were born on Yellow Creek in Graham County.

My father, whom I called Dad, had only a third grade education. He had started working in a logging camp at age 14. He was over six feet tall, muscular, left-handed and the best axeman with a double bitted axe I ever saw.

While I was young, he worked in logging camps and sometimes (during the winter months) he was gone for months at a time.

My mother, whom I called Mom, had finished the eighth grade. She was an excellent reader and she read many books to Dad and the children. She obtained the books at the public library in Bryson City and read to us at night while we all sat around the fireplace.

In addition to Mom's sisters, Aunt Dora and Aunt Annie, and her brothers, Uncle Jud and Uncle Charles, she had a brother, Uncle Perly Medlin, who lived in Robbinsville, in Graham County, with his wife, Aunt Hattie and their one child, a daughter.

In addition to his brother, Uncle Horace Hyde, Dad had a brother, Uncle Loftin Hyde. He and Dad were great buddies and they worked in the woods together. I knew Uncle Loftin for only a short time. But I do remember that he was humorous and it was great fun to be around him.

Unfortunately, he was killed in the woods by a falling tree when I was about three years old.

In addition to his sister, Aunt Ruth Hyde Walker, Dad had sisters Aunt Winnie Hyde Branton, Aunt Della Hyde Sherrill, Aunt Billie Hyde Gheen, Aunt Jean Hyde Helton and Aunt Maude Hyde Ogle. Aunt Winnie and her husband, Uncle Rob Branton, lived near us for a while and then moved to east Tennessee. Aunt Maude lived on Buckner Branch, about three miles from Emma Field, but later moved to Gaston County. Aunt Billie, Aunt Jean and Aunt Ruth moved to

Gaston County. Aunt Della Sherrill and her family moved to Virginia.

A dirt road led from Bryson City, the County seat of Swain County, down the Tuckaseigee River going west to Weeks Branch, Mountain Branch, Lands Creek, Peach Tree Creek, Cane Brake Branch, Noland Creek, Forney Creek, and on to Hazel Creek and Fontana. One way to our home in Emma Field was to take that road to Weeks Branch, turn up that branch by the home of Aunt Lizie Weeks, to the home of Aunt Lurie Ball. There another road came in from Bryson City which ran up Bryson Branch, then across a hill at Franklin Grove Baptist Church, down the hill west, past the homes of Henry Franklin, Uncle Ottis Franklin, Dave Franklin (and the road to Watkins Graveyard) Jackson Hollow and to the home of Aunt Lurie Ball. From there the dirt road went up by the houses of Lewis Ball, Al Ball, Oz Ball, Pat Hyde, Gram Pa Medlin and Jud Medlin and over the hill to Emma Field.

From Emma Field there had been a dirt road leading down the branch to Lands Creek and down Lands Creek to the home of Gram Pa Benjamin Hyde and Gram Ma Florence Penland Hyde, my Dad's parents, where there also lived with them their daughter, Aunt Ruth Hyde, and their son, Uncle Horace Hyde.

But a big slide below my first remembered home made it impossible to use it as a wagon road. We still used it as a trail or foot path and Dad used it to ride his horse. Gram Ma Hyde used it to walk to Bryson City—walking by our house—to visit her mother.

Gram Ma Hyde's house was about two miles from our house and was located on Lands Creek.

Back south, over the hill from Emma Field, Julius Ball lived up the hollow from his brother, Lewis Ball. We would often walk up a road by the home of Lewis Ball toward the home of Julius Ball—through a pasture—then turn up a trail and come back into the dirt road at Windy Gap.

There was also a "nigh" way up Jackson Hollow to get to Emma Field.

Julius Ball and his wife had several children. During the winter when there was snow on the ground, the boys would run rabbits through the snow. I could hear them yelling as they ran, following the rabbit tracks and giving directions to each other and I once heard one yell: "Here's where its been a 'wentin."

I knew what he meant.

North of Emma Field, and across a ridge, was the home of Jim

Bumgarner, later to become the home of Taylor Sherrill and his family. There was a trail across that ridge and by his house, then a dirt wagon road leading to the Lands Creek Road. That road came up Bryson Branch, through Sherrill's Gap down by the home of Joe Fee Shuler and down to the Lands Creek Road. On the Lands Creek Road the first house on the right, near the creek, was a house we lived in a short while. Then Frank Hyde and his wife, Jane Hyde, and later Carl Fox and his wife Maude Hyde Fox, and their daughter, lived there.

After we lived there a short while, we moved on up the creek to the old Jimmy Jenkins place, on a sixty acre tract of land, with a big house, a barn, a can house, a spring, a garden, a "tater" patch, a fenced-in pasture with acres of black berries and acres of woods where we got fire wood and wood for our wood-burning cook stove.

Dad bought all that for three hundred dollars during the Great Depression.

It was from the first house we lived in on Lands Creek that I walked up the creek and attended a one-room, one-teacher, seven grade school. Then I started walking out to Town School in Bryson City. I walked four miles each way each school day until I finished the eleventh grade and graduated from High School.

When I finished the seventh grade, I was the highest ranked boy in that grade and was crowned King.

My classmates in my Senior Year of High School named me "Sherlock Holmes" and as the boy most likely to succeed. I was also salutatorian.

Before moving to Lands Creek, we lived for a short time near Al Ball's house. That is where my little sister, Mary Alice, was born and lived only six weeks.

My first sister, Helen—two years younger than I—died at four while we were still in Emma Field. She died from a brain concussion, caused by a fall.

Also before moving to Lands Creek, my brother Walt and I attended school at Epps Springs, about four miles from our home. To get there we walked down Emma Branch to Lands Creek, down Lands Creek passing the home of Gram Pa and Gram Ma Hyde to the Tuckaseigee River and down the river to the school, near the mouth of Peach Tree Creek. That school, too, was a one room, one teacher, seven grade school. My brother, Walt, had first attended that school but caught pneumonia and missed an entire year of school.

As a result, we ended up both in the same class. And we continued in the same class through the ninth grade when Walt joined the Civilian Conservation Corps.

Walt and I and one other student walked out from Lands Creek to go to High School in Bryson City. No other student from Lands Creek went to High School with us. It was after I had finished High School before my younger brothers and sisters were enrolled there.

When Walt dropped out, so did the other student and, just as Walt and I did later on, joined the military service in World War II.

Back then, in speaking of relatives, I referred to grandparents, and even great grandparents, as Gram Pa and Gram Ma. All uncles were uncles, even if great. The same was true of aunts and great aunts. We referred to some non-relatives as Aunt or Uncle or Granny.

The sketches which follow are mostly from my boyhood years. Occasionally one must be linked up with some happening later along in life. And a few are about events that occurred shortly after I returned from the Pacific after World War II.

But I do not get into war stories or my time in military service, in college, in law school or my years of practicing law.

These stories have a different tone and I will come to them later.

2

The Old One

It was a great big world to a boy of two, even though it was just one creek and one valley in one county. But it lay in the Great Smokies, and mile after mile of mountain top and valley could be seen if you just climbed to the top of the hill. And you could see even more if you climbed a tree. Of course, you had to do that by yourself, when nobody else was around. For if they were around, they wouldn't let you. They'd keep scolding and pulling and pretty soon you'd just give it up to get rid of the noise and the pulling. Besides, there'd be another time. There always was a time when they weren't there.

And it was an old world, too. At least it seemed there were so many old things in it. Ancient, even. Like the one everybody called Gram Ma. There were some others that some called Gram Ma—it seemed like six or seven, at least—but only one that most everybody called Gram Ma, and sometimes "Gram Ma Garrett."

They later told me she was 103 when she died. They had a picture. It had her in it. And me, too. When I looked at the picture later, I knew who I was. Sitting there on her knees. She sure looked old. Old as the hills around us. A long straight nose she had, and very blue eyes, laughing eyes that were still clear and piercing after more than a century of looking. Straight out they looked. No glasses. None were needed, I guess. Other Gram Mas had glasses. But not that one. Not the old one. Born in 1825, they said—the year before Thomas Jefferson and John Adams died. But I didn't know who Thomas Jefferson was or John Adams for that matter. But the other folks seemed to know.

She had a hat on. But it seemed out of place to me. Maybe I didn't remember her that way. Somehow—vaguely—I could see her with her long hair rolled up in a knot. And a bright golden comb stuck in it. She sat by the fireplace. She didn't move much. Somehow I must have her mixed up. For I could see a pipe, a smoking pipe. That must be wrong. The other Gram Mas didn't have pipes. Gram Pa did. But he wore overalls and had a moustache. And he was big and tall and talked loud. He picked the banjo, too, and trotted me on his knee, and sang Jesse James and Li'l Liza Jane, and laughed big and loud, too.

I guess I was mixed up. But I couldn't get the blue eyes and the balled up hair and the old face and the pipe separated.

One of the Gram Mas called her "Mother," I think. And she called that one "Sarah Jane." But "Sarah Jane" was just another Gram Ma to me. Except she didn't have glasses. Nor a pipe. She sat and worked on the new quilts. And cooked. And things like that.

And then one day the old one was gone. I didn't see her anymore. Just the picture. And sometimes more than one picture. When the snow came and the wind blew through the walls and the cracks in the floor, I would lie on my belly on the floor in front of the fireplace. And I'd close my eyes and hold them tight and listen. Then I could see her again, at the fireplace, with the laughing blue eyes and the balled up hair and no hat. I just knew she was there and I was glad. I would keep my eyes shut a long time for when I opened them she wouldn't be there. I had done it before and she'd be gone. And I wouldn't feel good then. My stomach would hurt, like when I ate green apples.

And the wind sounded weird then and scary.

She never came back, except when I closed my eyes and the wind blew hard and the snow was cold on the ground. Or when I looked at the picture. Not even then did she really come back. It just seemed, then, that she might. And then I'd wish for the wind and the snow and the fireplace so I could close my eyes tight and see her.

Then the spring came, and the pretty flowers and the butterflies. And later came the bees that would sting when you stepped on them, especially when they were sitting on a green apple on the ground. And the birds were there — the blue birds and the jay birds that did so much clattering, and the red birds who told you when it was going to rain. And the squirrels came and built nests in the big apple trees.

Then things were new. And the old one wasn't there any more. The snow was gone and the wind didn't whistle so. I could close my eyes, but I wouldn't see her.

The fireplace was still there with no fire in it. And old Gram Ma was gone. It didn't seem right, but a lot of new things needed attention. My stomach didn't hurt so much any more when I couldn't see her. Besides, there were so many other Gram Mas. After a while it seemed that maybe there really hadn't ever been another one — with the pipe and the golden comb and the laughing blue eyes.

3

The Story the Old One
Left Me

But I knew she had lived with me. And there was definitely one thing The Old One left me. It was a story.

I remember sitting on her knees and listening to her story. She told me how the Smoky Mountains got their name.

The Old One was a great friend of the Cherokee Indians. She told me she was thirteen years old when the Cherokees were moved forcibly from their homes in the Smoky Mountains and taken to Oklahoma. Thousands died on the way.

But The Old One said that as they traveled west, they stopped each night and built camp fires.

In Swain County the wind blows from the west - over in Tennessee —and brings rain and snow.

The Old One said that the wind blew the smoke from the camp fires back to the mountains and there it settled.

And it would stay there until all the Cherokees came back home.

I know that scientists tell a different story. But I also know how that wind blows from the west. And I also know that in the Cherokee language, Tennessee (Tanasi) means "place where the Thunder Brothers play." That is in the west.

I believe the Old One.

4

The Shepherd Pup

Other things were happening, too. Dad was around more then. He would split the wood for the cook stove, and I helped carry it in. He would carry water from the spring. I'd try to help and usually got wet. I liked that.

Sometimes I could ride with him. It was a beautiful horse, a bay mare with a white star on her forehead. She wore a giant leather saddle that Dad put on her. And Dad wore spurs. They jingled when he walked.

Some days he would leave early, riding the mare and then be gone all day. I would stand and watch for him.

Fall came with bright golden days. The sky was so clear and blue. From a high hill you could see the whole world, almost. Only a smoky blue haze kept you from seeing the far mountains clearly.

One Sunday morning, bright and early, Dad saddled up the bay mare at the barn and rode her, single footing, down to the house. He got off and let me hold the bridle reins while he went into the house and back. He said he was going to Noland Creek and wouldn't be back until late.

I made it fine with him gone until after dinner. Then I worried Mom a lot by asking every few minutes when he would come back.

Finally I took up my vigil at the corner of the yard where I could see down the trail that led to Lands Creek and Peach Tree and beyond that to Noland Creek. I stayed there, looking west, until the sun started sinking behind the far mountains, a big red ball of fire which seemed to be setting the woods afire way back there.

Just before it finally sank from view, I saw some movement far down the trail. Then I saw the long shadow of a man and a horse coming over the rise. It was Dad and the bay mare.

I waited. As they reached the level, Dad reined in and let the mare blow. She turned a bit sideways and I could see the saddle a little plainer. It was a McClellan with a big horn in front. There was something else there now and Dad was holding it next to the horn — with one hand and, being left handed, he was holding the bridle reins in that hand. It wasn't his slicker up front; he had that rolled up and tied behind the saddle.

After a little while, he reined her around and the mare came pacing toward me. She was gaited and could "pace" as well as "single foot."

The sun was still in my eyes and I couldn't make out what Dad was holding on the front of the saddle. The mare came on and when she got to me, Dad reined in and leaned down from the saddle toward me. He had switched the reins to his right hand and he was holding something out to me with his left hand. It took me a second or two to make it out. In fact I was reaching for it before I finally knew what it was.

I took it in both arms, gently. It was the prettiest Shepherd pup I ever saw, about six weeks old, with bright eyes and warm and fluffy. As I took it, it didn't cry out or whine. It just looked up at me and started licking at my chin.

Shep had found a friend and a home.

"Can I keep it, Dad?"

"It's all yourn. I brought it to ye."

That started a friendship of sixteen years, covering all the boy days I had and then some.

He was to be my constant companion from then on. If Dad had allowed dogs in the house, I would have slept with him. But that was out. As it was we saw a lot of daylight together.

And that fall and winter I didn't have those mental pictures of the old Gram Ma so much. When the snow came and the wind blew through the walls and the cracks in the floor, I would lie in front of the fire and close my eyes and I could get a picture of Shep sleeping warm and comfortable in a corner of the barn which I had taken over for him. That made me feel good, looking toward tomorrow when we could hunt together or just go romping in the snow. I thought of the old Gram Ma now and then but not so often and it didn't seem so sad any more.

5

Chicken on Ice?

Dad was away that winter. He was in a logging camp on Roan Mountain, way over toward Tennessee and Virginia.

He had been gone for weeks. We were handling things at home, bringing in water, keeping the fires going, feeding the cow and the dogs. Mom milked the cow twice a day. Walt and I helped what we could.

Then we got lucky.

Dad's sister Ruth came to visit us, to stay overnight and to have fun with us. She was such a treat, a real delight.

She was always full of plans for doing something new, entertaining us all.

This time she came up with a great idea.

We had chickens, roosters and hens, mostly Domineckers but with a few white and red hens mixed in.

During good weather the chickens roosted in a holly tree and we fed them at the barn. During the day they would stay around the barn and scratch around for food.

But let a snowstorm or ice storm or blizzard come and they took up residence under that part of the house and porch that was up on stilts. The dirt yard was above a large portion of that and sloped down to the house.

When Aunt Ruth came that time, it came an ice storm. The dirt yard was covered in thick ice.

Aunt Ruth said we should feed the chickens by shelling ears of corn and throwing the corn out on the iced-over dirt yard.

We started. And so did the chickens. I never saw anything like it. The roosters and the hens would run out on the ice and try to run up the yard to get to a grain of corn. Some of the grains slid down the yard and these were easier to reach. But when a hen or rooster pecked at a grain of corn, it might catch it but inevitably the chicken fell and slid on the ice all the way down the yard.

We kept it up most of the day. We all were well entertained. And the chickens were not hurt and they did eat.

But I thought then that they all had to be a bit frustrated. I would have been if I'd been such a chicken on ice.

A Pheasant at Bay

Winter was on us. But, at least, Dad was home from the logging camp. Our summer and fall work was completed.

We had gathered in the crops and stored our canned berries, fruit and vegetables in the can house. Most of the cans were filled with blackberries. But we also had made jelly and apple butter by boiling it in the wash pot. We had made a barrel of sauerkraut and it was in the can house.

Also in the can house was a barrel of bleached apples. We had bleached the apples a layer at a time by burning a lid full of sulfur and letting the smoke bleach the apples, which we had peeled and sliced.

We also had several sacks full of dried beans, which we called leather britches. And we had dried apples and peaches and pickled beans. In the barn loft we had bushels of sweet potatoes laying on the floor in one layer but each not touching another.

We had stored our Irish potatoes by digging a shallow hole in the garden, lining it with straw, piling in bushels of potatoes and then covering them with a layer of straw and then covering that with dirt.

That was called a 'tater' hill. When we needed potatoes we dug away some dirt, removed some straw, took the potatoes we needed and then restored the straw and dirt.

We also had stored cabbage by plowing a deep row in the garden, pulling up the cabbage heads with the roots intact, then placing each head separately and upside down in the row and covering all with straw and dirt except for the very end of the root. That way the cabbage did not rot but stayed fresh up until about the end of

February. By that time we had used up about all the cabbage. It was always fresh and brittle when we took it out of the row where we had placed it. And it was about as white as snow.

We usually had the various parts of one hog which we raised and fattened each year, including ham and bacon and sausage.

Even so, we had to obtain money to buy things we couldn't raise: sugar, salt, black pepper, coffee, flour and lard.

And we ate mostly vegetables. We sometimes had chicken but not often.

So a wild fowl, such as a wild duck or a goose was a real treat but seldom did we have such.

That made it all the more important what happened to me and Shep one day that winter—on Christmas Eve.

There had been a medium snow but most of it had melted. There were still patches here and there and all the ground was wet, soft and some of it was muddy.

Mom sent me to the spring a little after noon to get a bucket of water.

Shep went with me.

The spring was about three hundred feet from the house, below the house and out of sight from the house. A ditch led from it to the main branch.

As I walked to the spring, Shep ran ahead of me. He stopped on the left side of the ditch, looked toward the ditch, moved over closer to it and started barking. I walked around the spring and walked to a spot back of Shep where I could see the upper bank of the ditch where his nose was aimed. That bank had caved in a small amount and there was a crevice under the bank, just back of the branch of water. And, behold! There stood a wild pheasant—at bay.

Shep kept on barking.

I backed off, out of sight of the pheasant, and I raced around the spring to the other side of the ditch. I walked to a spot near the bank, facing Shep across the branch. Then— notwithstanding the snow and the mud—I got down on my hands and knees and slowly crept forward. When I got to the edge of the bank I plunged forward, reaching my hands under the bank and grabbing the legs of the pheasant. I rolled over in the branch and, as the pheasant struggled, I rolled about in the water, the snow and the mud. But I held on. And finally I stood up, still holding the pheasant's legs with both hands.

With that Shep and I headed home. When we got near the house I yelled and Dad came out and met me. I handed him the pheasant.

At that point Dad took over.

Mom cooked the pheasant for supper.

And for years Shep and I received praise for the capture of that wild pheasant.

I never heard of anyone else catching one like that.

7

Come In From the Cold

Dad was a fox hunter. He loved Walker fox hounds. And over the years he owned scores of them.

But he also hunted possums and coons, rabbits and squirrels and sometimes went bear hunting.

So he dealt with many different breeds of dogs: Blue Ticks, Red Bones, Black and Tans, Plott Bear Hounds and Rabbit Beagles. But, except for Shep we never had a Shepherd or Collie and only one German Shepherd.

We called a German Shepherd a Police Dog.

And Dad found one and brought it home. His name was Frank.

At first we were all a little slow to get friendly with Frank. But soon we learned that he was our friend and had an instinct to protect us.

We started treating him as a favorite. It even got to the point that in bad weather Mom would let him in the house. No other dog got such good treatment, not even Shep.

But when it was bitter cold or there was snow, Frank would scratch on the front door and Mom would let him in. When he wanted out, he would scratch on the door and Mom would let him out.

That was mostly while Dad was away at some logging camp.

8

Do Dogs Count?

Dad trained his hunting dogs well. One way to train young dogs to tree possums was to have possums available to set loose, let them travel a short way, turn loose a trained dog first to follow the possum and then turn loose the young dogs to follow.

The dogs followed the trail of the possum by the scent and barked as they went. They would soon come so close to the possum that the object of the hunt would climb a tree to get out of the reach of the dogs. Then the dogs would circle the tree and bark. That was called "treeing" the possum.

You could catch a treed possum by shaking it out of the tree and grabbing it. We took a tow sack with us on a possum hunt and we would put the caught possums—sometimes two or three—in the sack and carry the sack home.

There we placed the captive or captives in a wooden barrel, usually located under a shed. The barrels had been made to hold sorghum molasses or whiskey or other commodities but Dad obtained three of them and used them for different purposes. One purpose was to hold captured possums and we would place as many as three in one barrel.

The possums could not get out of the barrel because the barrel was sloped in such a way that nothing could climb up the inside and get out.

Dad had instructed me and Walt on how to put in water and food for the possums and when he was gone we did that as a daily chore.

Frank, the police dog, took note of our performing the daily chore. After we had put water and food in the barrel, Frank would go to the barrel, place his front feet on the top of the barrel and peer down inside. Then he would back off and go off somewhere else or just lie down in the shed near the barrel.

One day Walt said to me: "What would Frank do if we stole one of the possums?"

I didn't have the answer but I suggested we try it out. We hit on a plan.

We fed and watered the possums and before Frank could get to the barrel, we took him behind the house and tied him up where he couldn't see the barrel or the chicken coop behind the barn. Then we took one possum out of the barrel and hid it in the chicken coop. Then we turned Frank loose.

Frank ran directly to the barrel. He looked in. Down he came and he started circling around and sniffing. In a little while he found the possum in the chicken coop. He went to the shed and lay down.

We took Frank back behind the house and tied him up. We then restored the possum to the barrel and turned Frank loose again. Directly to the barrel he went, peered in and then quietly lay down in the shed.

We ran through the same procedure taking out two possums and again taking out three possums. And we even tried leaving all three in the barrel and going through the same routine. It got so we didn't have to go through the part of placing water and food in the barrel while Frank watched. All we had to do was to tie him up and then turn him loose and he would check the barrel.

It never failed.

Walt and I were very impatient for Dad to get home so we could tell him that dogs could count. He came home and we told him so.

Dad had never heard such. But we went through the routine to prove it to him. When we finished, he believed it.

I never heard of anyone else owning a dog that could count. And maybe Frank was smarter than most other dogs.

But, whatever the case, it was great fun for me and Walt to go through it and especially to prove it to Dad.

9

You Don't Have to Fear the Unknown

I had barely reached five. I hadn't gone to school. I hadn't learned to read or write.

And I had listened to the ghost stories Granny Gouge told. I had learned to be afraid but I hadn't yet learned how to fight that.

And one night Dad really put me in a bind.

We then lived in the middle house in Emma Field. Our water bucket with a dipper and one wash pan were located on a porch next to the kitchen where we ate our meals.

We were sitting at the table eating supper. It was after dark.

Dad needed some water. He asked me to leave the table and to bring in the water bucket from the porch.

I responded. It was dark, I said. And I was afraid of the dark.

Dad got up. He led me outside to the porch, left me there and went back inside, locking the door.

I stood there.

I was afraid.

Then I grew angry.

I had thought that there were terrible things out there, things that could destroy me in a moment.

I had thought that there were giant monsters out there.

But as I stood there and thought about it I realized that I didn't really know what was out there. And then I came to the conclusion that whatever was out there I could handle it.

I knocked on the door and said to my Dad: "Dad, I don't know what's in the dark but I can whup anything out there." Dad opened the door and let me in. I have never been afraid of the dark since then.

10

Creaking Trees

It wasn't long after that that I had another after dark experience. This time, though, it was not really so black dark.

It was in late fall. And it was after dark.

But there was a full moon. And the sky was partly cloudy, the wind was blowing hard and clouds were drifting around. Sometimes when no clouds blocked the moon, it was almost as bright as day. Then the cloud would move and it was darker.

I was going home from Aunt Annie's. She and Uncle Ottis lived about two miles from our home in Emma Field. I took the trail up Jackson Hollow to get home.

The trail led up a ridge. As I climbed I suddenly heard a loud creaking noise. I couldn't imagine what it was. It stopped. I walked a few steps. There it was again. It was behind me. I walked back a few steps. I heard it again. This time it sounded as though it was above me.

I walked back a little more and stopped. The creaking sound came again. It was closer to me and above me.

I kept thinking of witches and those ghost stories Granny Gouge had told us.

But I stood and I kept looking. Then I heard the sound just as I saw the tops of two trees go in opposite directions.

I looked more closely.

Then it became clear to me.

Two trees had grown up pushing against each other. Near the top of each they came together. As the wind blew they would rub against each other. That made the sound.

I was glad I had stopped and figured it out. That is one way of getting over being scared.

11

Knowing Who Is Boss

I knew long before I was five years old that I had to follow the orders of Dad. That was clear.

With Mom it was also true but not quite so strict.

I hadn't yet gone to school where I would learn to mind the teacher, the bus driver (when I rode a bus) and other older people, like the janitor.

So it was a real problem to me at five years of age to have my Gram Pa Hyde say that he would give me a whupin'.

Gram Pa Hyde chopped fire wood for the fireplace and stove wood for the wood burning cook stove. It was all done with a double bitted axe. He didn't have anyone to help him cut wood with a cross cut saw. Walt and I cut our wood that way for years. It made the whole task much easier. Gram Pa Hyde, like most mountain men, was very careful with his axe. He kept it razor sharp, using a grind stone and sometimes a file. And he was very careful what he chopped. Above all, he never let the blade hit the ground. To him that was a major sin.

I know. I committed that sin in his presence.

Our family was visiting my grandparents on a Sunday after we went to church at the Rock Creek Baptist Church. Mom and Gram Ma Hyde were fixing dinner, the noon day meal.

Her house had a long wide porch in front, set up on stilts. The porch covered the full length of the house. At each end of the porch was a wide set of steps made from split logs. There were seven steps on each end.

The wood yard was a few feet from those steps, above the smoke house and close to a branch that came down from Coon Cove where there was a pasture and an eight acre corn field.

In the wood yard was a large chopping block which was kept secure there by four wooden stakes driven in the ground to hold it.

Gram Pa Hyde chopped his wood there, and often left his axe chopped into the chopping block.

It was that way that Sunday.

Gram Pa Hyde was standing on the top step of the porch near the wood yard. Dad was standing at the bottom of the steps near the wood yard. I was at the chopping block looking at the axe. My brother Walt was near by.

To get a better look I took the handle of the axe in my hands and pulled the axe out of the chopping block.

But the axe was heavy and I dropped it. One bit drove into the ground.

They all saw it.

Gram Pa Hyde looked at me and then at Dad and said: "Ervin, I'm gonna whup that boy."

That astounded me.

It would be all right for Dad to punish me. But not someone else.

I reached out and picked up a rounded off creek rock about the size of a hen egg.

Gram Pa Hyde took one step toward me on the porch steps. I drew back my arm and threw the rock.

Even at that age, I was known as an accurate rock thrower.

The rock hit Gram Pa Hyde just above his right eye. Blood came out. Gram Pa Hyde stopped.

My Dad said to his Dad: "Dad, I'll take care of it. It's up to me."

I agreed.

And it didn't bother me at all that Dad cut a switch and gave me a whipping on the lower back and upper legs.

I knew that I should not have dropped the axe.

I also knew who my boss was. And it stayed that way. That suited me.

12

A Copper to Church

I was five years old. My brother Walt was seven, our little sister, Helen, was three and our brother Carroll was one year old.

We all went to church on Sunday. We then attended Franklin Grove Baptist Church. Gram Pa Medlin drove a one horse buggy to church and of course, Gram Ma Medlin rode in the buggy. There was also room in the buggy for Mom, Helen and Carroll. Walt and I would walk to church.

But Gram Pa Medlin was helpful to us also. Each Sunday he gave each one of us a penny to put in the collection plate at church. He called a penny a copper.

It was his effort to teach us about tithing to the church. The Depression was then upon us and a penny was valuable.

But we did as he said. We gave it.

And perhaps it taught us a lesson. Give what you can even if it is very little.

To us it was all that we had. But perhaps I missed the point.

13

Fum! Fum!

Dad told us this story.

He and a cousin named John Bee were over on Noland Creek. They stopped by the house of a friend and were talking to him in the yard.

Some of their friend's children were playing records on a phonograph in the house.

At that time TV had not been invented. No one in our part of the world had electricity. Few had ever heard a radio. And many had never heard records played on a phonograph. Apparently John Bee was one of those.

As they left, going homeward, John Bee said to Dad: "What was that dern thing making that dern noise?" "What noise?" said Dad. John Bee replied: "That Fum, Fum, Diddeley, Fum, Fum, Fum."

14

One Dog Bite—Free

We were then living in the middle house in Emma Field.
My sister, Helen, loved to play outside on a clear, warm day in a sand box Dad had made for her.

Our police dog, Frank, usually lay under the porch, back of the sand box.

Gram Pa Hyde would walk by our house when going to town or when going to visit his daughter, Maude, on Buckner Branch.

He always had a walking stick. He had made it himself and it had a curved handle which he held as he used it to help him walk.

Helen was in the sand box. Gram Pa Hyde came along, stopped and playfully hooked the handle around her neck.

At that moment, Frank came out and grabbed his knee with his teeth. Gram Pa yelled and backed off and Frank turned loose.

Dad was nearby.

Gram Pa said to Dad: "Ervin, we ought to shoot that dog." "No" said Dad. "He was doing right. He was taking care of Helen."

That ended the matter.

I noticed that Gram Pa Hyde was much more careful after that when he was around Frank.

15

Radio or No

Aunt Annie Medlin Franklin had one story she loved to tell about me. It was true and I couldn't deny it.

At that time few people had a radio. In fact, it was a while later and after we had moved to Lands Creek, that I started going with other boys and men over to Bryson Branch to listen to the championship boxing on the radio.

Someone had said that Tom Lowe—who lived on Lands Creek next above Gram Pa Hyde and operated a corn mill there—had a radio.

Aunt Annie asked me if Tom Lowe had a radio. I replied that my Dad said he did but I couldn't swear to it. I think she told that story to point out that I needed proof before I would admit anything.

I didn't see anything wrong with that.

I still don't.

16

One Who Bites Is Hidden

Dad was the best axeman I ever saw, the best marksman I ever saw and the most careful man with animals I ever saw.

But we all are human. I suppose that he, too, fell short of the mark on occasion.

At least I saw that on one occasion he did so.

And his doing so taught me a lesson: When you can't see, don't assume anything.

Dad and I were cutting wood. Shep jumped a rabbit and the rabbit and Shep came running by us. We both saw the rabbit run to the trunk of a hollow tree and run inside the tree.

Dad and I went over to the tree. Shep was bouncing around there looking at the hole in the hollow tree and barking. He had the rabbit treed.

Dad walked up to the tree, bent down on one knee and reached his left hand into the tree. Instantly he drew his hand back out, uttering a strong word.

His hand was bleeding. Something had bitten his hand.

Dad then employed the traditional method of pulling an animal out of the tree. He cut a stick and inserted it into the tree, twisting it as he pushed it in. In a moment the twisting stopped and he pulled the stick out. The stick was twisted into the hair and skin of a squirrel and Dad pulled the squirrel out.

That was what had bitten him. It was not the rabbit because rabbits won't bite you.

He released the squirrel, even though it was the culprit, and he inserted the stick again, twisted it around and pulled out the rabbit.

The rabbit had simply run into a place already occupied by the squirrel and the squirrel did the natural thing when Dad put his hand in the tree.

Dad didn't tell me anything.

But I got the point. I don't put my naked hands into a hollow tree without knowing what is in there.

Or anywhere else.

17

Eagles Claw and Cats Gnaw

My great grandmother Sara Jane Garrett Penland lived into her late nineties. She was active to the end. She cooked and sewed and canned black berries after she was ninety five.

My wife, Kitty, and I would go visit her and she loved giving cans of black berries to our daughters.

She told me many stories going back to the days of the War Between The States.

But the best one she ever told me had happened when she was about six years old.

Her family then lived on Lands Creek, on the farm next upstream from the home of her daughter and Gram Pa Hyde. At the time she told me the story that place was occupied by Tom Lowe, who operated a corn mill there.

I knew the place well. The house she had lived in was still there. The spring her family had used was still the spring used by the Lowe family. Between the house and the spring was a large flat rock about two feet high, four feet long and two feet wide, located next to the trail which led from the house to the spring.

When she was six years old her family had attended church on a Sunday in the Spring. They returned home and her mother was preparing dinner.

She was out in the yard, looking toward the spring. The family cat was a large yellow tom cat. She saw him sleeping on the large flat rock near the spring.

Suddenly there was a shadow and then a large bird -an eagle-swooped down and, with its claws, grabbed the tom cat and carried it into the air.

She watched. She was amazed.

The eagle and the cat fought. Fur and feathers filled the air as the two went higher, hundreds of feet into the air.

And then the lift upward stopped. The cat had managed to cut the eagle's throat and killed it. But the eagle still held on to the cat and they both dropped hundreds of feet to the ground, landing in front of Gram Ma.

The fall killed the cat. There they lay in front of her, both dead.

She yelled for her mother who came and she, too, was astonished.

It is hard to imagine the great effect that had on Gram Ma Penland. But almost a century later she recalled it and could tell it with all the details and could show all the awe and astonishment she experienced when it happened.

And I could feel it, too, as I stood on the very spot where it had happened.

18

Revenuer

Somehow the government passed a law that required people to pay a tax on whiskey, brandy, wine, beer or home brew which they might make out of their corn or apples or peaches or other crops or fruits they might grow on their farms. Mountain folks didn't like that but they were put in some jeopardy by officers hired by the government to collect revenue on such products.

Those officers were referred to as "revenuers."

I didn't know that when I was five years old.

But some years later I learned that there was a general rule that if a revenuer took part in the manufacture or consumption of such products he couldn't arrest and testify against the offender.

I didn't know any of that at the time.

But I did know that Dad had made some mighty fine home brew in a crock setting on a table in our kitchen. I knew because Dad would let me drink part of a tin cup full once in a while. It was great. I loved it. There wasn't anything around that tasted better.

And I didn't know that a man who was married to a cousin of Dad was a revenuer, a man named Charlie.

Late one summer evening Dad and I were out in the yard. The sun was setting in the west and the sunset was beautiful.

I was looking west. Suddenly there was a shadow and then came riding a man on a beautiful bay mare. She had a star in her forehead. And the saddle and the bridle were lined with beautiful silver. The mare had white on her ankles. She was beautiful.

The man rode up and stopped. He and Dad started talking.

I walked around looking at the horse and the saddle and the bridle. I was so pleased.

And I thought to myself that I ought to offer to the man something I really liked.

I stopped and I pulled on his pants leg and I said: "Mister, would you like some good home brew?"

"Dang" said Dad. Then he said: "Git down, Charlie, and come on in."

I didn't know that Charlie was the revenuer. Dad took him in and Charlie drank a cup of home brew. He said it was good. Then he left.

Then Dad explained to me that I should not tell about the home brew and that they could send him to jail for making it and that I wouldn't see him again if they did.

I never spoke about the home brew to anyone again. I just enjoyed it when I could.

19

What Big Oranges

During those early years we provided for ourselves on our place about everything we needed. We had apples and grapes and grew watermelons and mush melons. We picked blackberries and huckle berries and goose berries and raised some strawberries in our garden.

And, in fact, at Christmas time each year we managed to get a few oranges which were grown in some foreign state.

But that was about all.

When I was four years old I had never seen or heard of a grapefruit.

Aunt Annie Medlin and Uncle Ottis Franklin had married and were living with her parents.

They had acquired some grapefruit for Christmas and had thrown out the hulls into the hollow near the road.

Walt and I were walking by the house when we saw the grapefruit hulls. I didn't know Uncle Ottis was near by and listening and I said: "Good gosh, Walt! What big oranges over there."

Uncle Ottis told that on me for years. And I never denied it. After all, it was true.

20

The Cow With the All Overs

Mountain folks- just like most other isolated people- have a dialect all their own.

Of course, I didn't know that when I was growing up because I was isolated with them.

In describing a man in a hurry, my folks would say he was "worried." If a person were highly fretful, the word to describe that person was "tetchious," probably from "toucheous," meaning not wanting to be touched.

An unusually nervous person was said to have the "all overs." I suppose that could have come from the fact that such a person would shake all over at times.

When I was about four years old, I heard that term used in a highly unusual way.

Gram Pa Hyde knew that wilted wild cherry leaves, when eaten by a cow, could make that cow very sick or even kill that cow. He and other mountain folks were very careful not to cut and leave wild cherry limbs in a cow pasture while the leaves were still green.

But on one occasion, Gram Pa Hyde was not careful enough.

He had a sled road leading up Coon Cove from his house to a corn field on the left side of the Cove. Along the right hand side of that cove was his cow pasture made of barbed wire nailed to stakes. There were three strands of wire and a cow or horse or mule could stick its head between the strands and eat grass or weeds or leaves along the edge of the road.

Some wild cherries were growing along that fence and the edge of the road. The limbs were growing out over the road and Gram Pa Hyde cut off those protruding limbs which fell along the edge of the road.

He didn't know it until after one of his cows became very sick—and was treated and cured—that she had poked her head through that fence and eaten a great amount of wild cherry leaves after they had wilted.

All he knew at that time was that one of his cows became very sick after he brought her out of the pasture to his barn.

That cow was bloated. Her stomach was extended so much that she looked like a balloon that kept getting bigger and bigger. Finally she lay down on the ground and lolled her tongue out.

It appeared she was dying.

Gram Pa was watching her. My brother Walt and I were there, along with Uncle Horace. Gram Pa sent Walt and Uncle Horace to the home of a friend who lived at the head of Peach Tree Creek. He was totally illiterate but he was said to be very good at treating sick animals.

It was a long trip. Gram Pa and I waited.

Finally Walt and Uncle Horace came back, bringing the friend of Gram Pa with them, all walking.

The gentlemen took a good, close look at the cow, lying on her side with her tongue lolling out.

Then he reached into the right hip pocket of his overalls and pulled out something made of metal. He placed that instrument between two ribs of the cow and stuck it into her. He held it there a while and then removed it.

I could hear air or gas escaping from the cow's entrails. It made a big noise for several minutes.

Then the cow lifted her head and took her tongue back. She then moved around on the ground and finally stood up. Her sides were no longer swollen and extended.

She lolled her tongue around her mouth. She shook her head.

Then she started walking—slowly. She moved out to a patch of grass and started eating the grass.

She was well!

Gram Pa then asked his friend if the cow would be all right and the reply was affirmative.

Then Gram Pa asked him what he owed him for his help, which included at least a ten mile round trip.

The friend replied that it would be a quarter.

Gram Pa paid him.

Then Gram Pa asked him what was wrong with the cow.

The friend then demonstrated that he did not want to give away any secrets of his acquired knowledge.

He replied: "Wuh' Wuh! By Ned! She had the all overs."

That was all he ever said about it.

Gram Pa discovered very soon after his friend left that a whole bunch of the wilted wild cherry leaves had been devoured. It was then obvious what had made the cow sick.

Still, I found it interesting that she was diagnosed merely as highly nervous but cured in a most unusual manner.

21

The Guidance of Gram Ma Hyde

I didn't figure it out until Gram Ma Hyde was gone and I was past forty years old. But I know now. She led me to be a lawyer. But she never said so or mentioned the subject to me or ever made any suggestion about it. I guess that is why I missed it for so long.

Gram Ma Hyde was always working except when she visited her mother, my Great Gram Ma Penland in Bryson City.

We lived between Gram Ma Hyde's home and Bryson City. She would come to our house on her way to her mother's house, using a trail along the branch that ran into Lands Creek.

She would stop at our house and ask Mom if I could go with her. Mom always agreed.

That went on for about six years, from my age of five to eleven. It happened about twice a year. I didn't know it then but later learned that Court was held in Bryson City only twice a year.

Gram Ma was a fast walker. I could barely keep up with her as we walked to town. But I did.

And when we reached Bryson City, Gram Ma Hyde always took me to the Court House and to the second floor where she had me to sit in a seat in the back row of the Court Room. There she would leave me and be gone for a long time but would come back and get me and take me with her to Gram Ma Penland's house. My visit there would be short and then came the long walk back home.

While I was in the Court House, I listened to the lawyers pick juries, present witnesses and argue to the Judge and jury.

I could hear the lawyers make a statement and then say to the Judge: "I move to strike that from the record."

And the motion would be granted and the whole matter would be stricken out as if it had never happened.

I thought how wonderful that was. Here the lawyer had done wrong —he had sinned—and then he had gained forgiveness.

What instant redemption.

That may have been what led me to become a lawyer.

Gram Ma Hyde and I never discussed those matters. I never mentioned it to Dad or Mom. All I did was to go with her and, when she left me at the Court House, wait for her return.

Over the years I learned what to expect from the lawyers and the Judge. I found all of it to be interesting and much of it to be very exciting.

Still, it was long after I finished law school, passed the bar examination and started practicing law before I ever thought of or made any connection between my choice of a profession and the acts of Gram Ma Hyde when I was a mere lad.

But now I know she planned it that say. I'm glad it worked. She lived long enough to see it work but still never mentioned it to me. I guess she knew I would figure it out some day.

22

A Bright Issue Coming Up

Dad loved corn liquor. It could be that at times he loved it a little too much.

So did Uncle Fide.

Dad told me on one occasion when he got home to Emma Field that he and Uncle Fide had been together that day.

They had been drinking some corn liquor and were on their way home. They took the nigh way up Jackson Hollow. But they both got sleepy and they lay down in the leaves along the trail and both went to sleep. They slept until about sundown when the sunset was beautiful in the west.

Uncle Fide woke up and said to Dad: "Where are we?" Dad was already awake and he answered: "Uncle Fide, we died and went to hell."

Uncle Fide looked to the west and replied: "I believe you're right. I see a bright issue comin' up over there."

23

Make No Mistakes

I started going to school in the fall when I was six years old. The Depression was about as bad as it would get. Money was scarce everywhere.

I had never owned a pencil. But Dad looked out for me. He bought me a penny pencil at the store in town and brought it home. He told me about it and started to hand it to me.

Then he paused, holding the pencil in one hand. He reached into the front pocket of his overalls and pulled out his long pocket knife which he always carried.

He opened his knife and, holding the penny pencil in the other hand, he first sharpened the pencil and then, turning it, he cut off the eraser from the other end.

He handed the pencil to me, sharpened but with no eraser.

He said to me: "Don't make any durn mistakes."

I took the pencil. I thanked him for it.

I learned to write with that pencil.

But I was not able to follow Dad's command completely.

I made mistakes. I still do. I fall short of the mark even as the Apostle Paul admitted he had done.

But I believe that because of that incident I was a little more careful and perhaps—just perhaps—I made fewer mistakes than I would have made without it.

24

Riding Sideways

Uncle Lum had moved into the house above us in Emma Field. He had a young bull. It grazed grass above his house in a hollow. There was a trail from that hollow across a ridge and through the woods to our corn field in another hollow above our barn. That bull would sometimes follow that trail to our corn field and eat our green corn stalks.

Dad wasn't home, so Walt and I were in charge of such matters. We decided to put a stop to that.

We got a long cow rope, made a large loop in one end, laid that end in the trail and tied the other end around a nearby oak tree uphill from the loop.

We kept a watch out on the trail for two days but the bull didn't show. On the third day we were back there again and we heard the bull coming along the trail. We hid behind the oak tree.

The bull walked by until his two front feet were in the loop of the rope. We then jerked the rope and the loop went up around the front legs of the bull. At the same time we both yelled real loud. The bull jumped and tried to run but the rope grew tight around his front legs and he fell to the ground, flipping over as he went. He struggled to get up but he couldn't.

Walt and I had not made final plans on what to do when we caught the bull.

The bull was not big; in fact he was just a yearling, as we called such. While the bull lay there we talked about what to do.

My Home is in the Smoky Mountains

Finally, I said we ought to "break him in" to ride as Dad often did with new, young horses.

Dad had a large McClellan saddle in the barn. It was about all I could carry.

But I ran to the barn and got it while Walt kept watch over the bull. We managed to get the bull to stand up, still with the rope around his front legs. Then we put that saddle on him and buckled it on tight.

I got into the saddle.

We had another small rope and I told Walt to tie the stirrups together with the rope under the bull's belly. He did so.

Walt then untied the rope looped around the bull's front legs.

There was no bridle on the bull's head. In fact, I had no way at all to guide him.

He jumped and burst into a run down the trail.

Then he cut through the woods and into a black berry patch and through more bushes.

Neither Walt nor I knew that the skin on the back of a bovine—cow or bull—was so loose that it could turn from one side to the other. Later Gram Pa Hyde told us that.

That may explain what happened to that saddle. It went from back to side to side and I was holding on to the horn, going with it.

I was yelling, too, and crying out for help.

Walt was running after us. The bull ran to the top of a hill and stopped just as Walt got there. It was breathing heavily.

I jumped out of the saddle and off of the bull. Walt cut the small rope under the bull's belly with a pocket knife and jerked the saddle buckle free. The saddle fell off.

The bull then moved on but much more slowly.

I don't believe we taught that bull very much.

But I learned to ride sideways about as well as anyone I have ever seen in my life.

25

Tarzan Falling

The boys played Tarzan in the trees. Our wooded hills did not form a jungle. And although there were a few wild grape vines here and there among the trees, most of these were found along the creeks. We didn't swing on vines.

Still, we would climb one tree and jump from one tree limb to the limb of another tree.

You could climb a yellow pine and get it to swing over toward another tree. That was a good way to travel.

And what we were doing amounted to a race, to see who could travel the longest distance in the shortest time.

I took part. I enjoyed it. And, then, one day I learned about young yellow poplar. In my zeal I had climbed a tall yellow pine and got it to bend toward the next tree, a yellow poplar. I swung out and grabbed that poplar near its top with both hands. I was then about fifteen feet above the ground.

But I didn't stop. I didn't even slow down. The poplar broke. I fell to the ground. I didn't become unconscious. But I lost my breath.

There I lay.

The other boys got out of the trees and came running. They picked me up and started walking me along a trail. I could use my legs as they held me, but I couldn't breathe.

They walked me about thirty steps before I caught my breath. We stopped and I came back to normal.

I had no broken bone nor any permanent injury. But I did get a permanent prejudice. I still don't like yellow poplar trees—or anything else that breaks that easily.

26

An Indian Hammer Found

Most homes had in them a few Indian arrows found by family members. Most of these were about the same size and made from a flint rock, usually white but sometimes red. These were the size used for arrow heads.

Gram Pa Hyde had one very small arrow made from black flint. Uncle Rob Branton, who lived in east Tennessee, told me that that was for a small bird arrow and came from Tennessee. There were no black flint rocks close around where we lived.

Only once, however, did I see a hammer made from stone.

I found it myself.

Dad and I were walking back home from a trip over to Peach Tree, an area now totally in the Great Smoky Mountains National Park.

We turned up by the house of Uncle Fide Hyde to follow a trail which led through a low gap to Possum Hollow and down that hollow to Lands Creek.

We were about one hundred feet above and east of Uncle Fide's house. Uncle Fide had been mending or improving that trail. He had dug it out some and made the path more even.

As we walked along, Dad was ahead of me on the trail, and at age five I was considerably shorter than my tall Dad. Maybe that let me see the ground a little more closely.

At any rate, I noticed something not quite common which had been dug out of the hill as Uncle Fide made his improvement.

I stopped and picked it up. It was a stone hammer. It was about three inches long, perfectly round on each end with the ends almost one inch in diameter. The middle was about one and a half inches in diameter and had a perfectly round hole for a handle. It was even and smooth all over with no breaks in it. The hole for the handle was filled with dirt. I showed it to Dad. He looked it over and took a stick and punched out the dirt in the handle hole.

Dad had never seen one like it. Neither had Gram Pa Hyde or anyone else we asked.

We took it home. It became one of my prized possessions.

Unfortunately it was lost sometime after I left home for the Navy in World War II.

All I have now is the fond memory of it.

27

Under a Rock—A Spear

I also have fond memories of one other discovery of my own. That was a long flint spear head and I found it, too. I found it much closer home.

While we were living in the middle house in Emma Field, we had a corn field which ran westward over a low ridge northwest of our house.

It lay partly in a hollow which ran down to the branch below our house and garden. The road to the lower house was just above the branch and the area was wooded for about two hundred feet between that road and the corn field.

About twenty feet above the woods and the lower edge of the corn field lay a large flint rock. It was about five feet long, two feet wide and two feet thick. It was never moved that I knew of. We just plowed around it. And hoed around it.

I don't know what prompted me to want to turn it over except for childish curiosity about what might be found under it. And for the life of me I can't remember why I ever thought I could turn it over by myself.

Dad had a peavy. That was used for rolling logs and most logs were not near the size of that rock and didn't weigh as much.

A peavy has a wooden shaft or stake fitted into a metal which has a sharp end, extending from the end of the shaft. A pivoting hook arm is fastened to the metal and swings so that it can be adjusted to fit the size of the object desired to be moved.

I tried the peavy on the rock. Even though I could get the hook under the edge of the rock, I couldn't come close to lifting up the rock.

I then took a hoe and dug out the dirt under the upper edge of the rock so that I had about a two inch hole running back about six inches under the rock.

Then I carried a large rock over to the upper side and, placing it near the large flint rock, I inserted the peavy between them and used it as a lever. I also brought smaller rocks and when I was able to lift the rock at all, I would push a smaller rock under the large flint with my foot.

It took a long time and I probably flirted with danger, but I finally rolled the rock over.

And there where the large flint rock had been so long, clearly exposed, was the largest flint spear head I had ever seen. I took it home.

Nobody around there had ever seen one like it before.

I placed it along with the rock hammer.

Alas, they probably stayed together. I couldn't find it after the War.

28

Stray Geese

I have been told that each fall flocks of wild geese fly south along our sea coast on their way to places with milder winters. I have never been there to observe that.

And only once have I ever observed such a flight in the Smoky Mountains.

Older folks had never seen the like either but they explained to me that the winds had blown the geese west and that is why they flew south over our mountains.

It was an almost unbelievable sight. The whole sky was covered with flying geese. And the geese were fairly close to the ground, flying just high enough to get over the ridge.

It happened on a Saturday afternoon. It was a sunny day. But the flock cut off entirely any view of the sun.

Dad was home. He walked out in the yard with me and Mom and Walt and Helen and Carroll. He watched a while and then he went back into the hall where he had his double barreled shotgun laying on hooks above the door.

He came back out and walked past us a few yards. He then fired one barrel and in a few moments fired the other barrel of the shotgun.

As each shot sounded, a goose fell. But they didn't fall straight down on us. They went forward and fell near the branch in our pasture.

By the time they hit the ground, Walt and I were running to get them. Each was dead. We carried back one each.

We had goose for supper and enjoyed it on Sunday, too.

I never saw anything like it again.

29

A Turn of Corn

Man may not live by bread alone. But when it came to bread, mountain folks lived mostly on corn.

We raised our own corn. We planted it, plowed it, hoed it and harvested it.

When it came time to harvest, we first pulled the blades off the stalk below the ears of corn.

We cut off the tops above the ears. The blades we rolled in bundles and tied those bundles with other blades of corn.

We put the tops in bundles or shafts of corn and also tied them with blades of corn.

We then stacked the tops around a stack pole, keeping the tops standing up and we placed bundles of corn blades above the tops and then topped it off by tying blades around the stack pole. That constituted a stack of fodder.

We pulled the ears, shucks and all, hauled them in a sled to the barn and stored them in the crib, a room on the ground floor of the barn where the corn could dry out.

We then shucked the corn ears, storing the shucks for feeding the cattle. Some folks kept their shucks with which to fill their bed ticks. We didn't do that. We used straw for that.

As corn was needed for feeding cattle or for shelling and feeding the chickens, we got it from the crib. We also shelled corn for making hominy and stored the hominy in a barrel in the can house.

But the greatest use of corn was for making meal. Meal was used for making corn bread, corn mush, corn meal gravy and corn pones.

But the greatest was for bread and we ate corn bread at least twice a day. We also kept our dogs alive on corn bread.

We would usually shell a bushel of corn at a time, pour it into a white cloth sack, which we called a meal sack, and carry that to the local corn mill for grinding. Then the meal was placed back into the meal sack, carried home and stored in a wooden meal chest.

Dad had always carried our corn to the corn mill of Tom Lowe located near Tom Lowe's house. That house was the next house up Lands Creek from the house of Gram Pa Hyde. It was also the house where Gram Ma Penland lived when she saw the eagle and the cat fight it out and kill each other.

Finally the time came for me to carry my first "turn of corn" to the mill house. Dad laid the bag of corn on my back and I carried it to Tom Lowe's mill. It was only half the usual amount Dad took for grinding.

When I got there, Tom Lowe was in his mill house. I set the sack of corn down and told Mr. Lowe that Dad sent me to get the corn ground.

Mr. Lowe opened the sack and poured the corn into a round wooden half bushel tub. Then he took a metal scoop with a wooden handle, and scooped out a scoop full and poured that scoop of corn into a large barrel.

I had been told that the term "turn of corn" meant that if other people were at the mill to get their corn ground when you arrived, you had to wait in line for your "turn" in order to get your corn ground.

But no one had told me about the miller taking his "toll" out of your corn before he ground the remainder into meal and by using a scoop to measure the toll.

I didn't know what Mr. Lowe was doing. I thought that he was stealing my corn.

I grabbed the empty sack, burst out of the door and headed for home, running as fast as I could.

When I got to our yard Dad was standing outside. I paused and caught my breath.

Dad said to me: "What in the Dickens is going on?"

I replied: "Dad, he stole my corn."

Dad explained the matter to me and then I understood the "toll."

I took other "turns" of corn to the mill but I understood it better then.

30

Owls and Chickens Don't Mix Well

Rudy Maynor lived near the head of Lands Creek. He had a son, Carl Maynor, who was a grown up young man while I was still a boy. We became friends. We would meet and talk at church. And we always spent some time together on Decoration Day.

Decoration Day was a very important day to all the folks I knew when I was growing up.

That was the day when we all gathered at the graveyard and paid respect to our kin folks and friends who had gone on to another world.

I didn't know it when I was very young but when I grew up and checked it out I found out that it was always celebrated one week before Memorial Day.

The graveyard where most of my kin folks and friends were buried was Watkins Graveyard. It is located east of my birthplace, near the home of Dave Franklin and within the boundary of the old grant my Gram Pa Garrett took out.

Many of my kin folks on my mother's side are buried in cemeteries on Hazel Creek, all within the Great Smoky Mountains National Park. We have some difficulty nowadays getting to visit those graveyards.

But, as a boy, I went each Decoration Day to Watkins Graveyard.

When I was six years old I went to Decoration Day. Carl Maynor was there. He saw me and he came over and we struck up a good conversation. While we were talking he told me that recently he had caught an owl. He said he had it in a box out in a buggy which his Dad and Mother had driven to the graveyard.

I was very interested. I had learned from Dad that owls were a great enemy of chickens. That is why our chickens just loved to roost in a holly tree which had green leaves all year long. That way the owls could not swoop in and catch them. Owls would do that when they could, killing the chickens and eating them.

My interest was aroused because I had noticed some of the chickens not yet grown were getting into Mom's garden and picking at her tomatoes and digging up her other vegetables. This was so even though we had a fence around the garden to keep the chickens out. The fence was made from split pine slabs which we called a paling fence. The slabs were nailed to stakes and the slabs were close together to keep the chickens out.

Even so the chickens got in.

But I thought that if I had an owl at my command I could do better than any paling fence.

When I explained that to Carl he gave me the owl.

What a gift!

I took it home.

And I kept it in good shape. I fed it and I watered it.

And I waited until the right time.

Then one day I saw a pullet in Mom's garden. A pullet is a young female chicken, not yet a hen. She was pecking at one of the tomatoes.

I took the owl out of the box. I had a long string tied around its legs so that I could toss it and hold on to the string.

I tossed it at the pullet. It hit the pullet.

To my amazement the pullet's neck suddenly stretched about one inch longer than normal. To my utter amazement its neck continued to stand out at least one inch longer.

I pulled the owl back. The pullet ran. But her neck did not go back to normal. It remained stretched out at least one inch longer than normal.

Her neck never got any shorter. I observed it for days and I can confirm that it stayed at least one inch longer.

I have presented this matter to several professors but I have never received a reasonable explanation of what happened.

I don't know the answer.

But I do know that chickens and owls don't mix well.

31

Those Turkeys: Can Anything Be So Dumb?

Walt and I were trying to make some money. We didn't know the first thing about economics but we were still trying to make money so we could buy some things we wanted and didn't have.

Maybe we were at least in line with the often stated American dream.

We decided to raise turkeys.

We didn't know the first thing about turkeys but we set out anyhow.

We got us a turkey hen and we set her over a nest of eggs. We were lucky. The eggs hatched. So far we were doing fine.

And then the young ones started to run around outside.

That was fine until the first rain came.

That is when they ran out, lifted their heads and opened their mouths. Half of them were drowned while we watched.

Walt and I quit raising turkeys. We couldn't believe that anything could be so dumb. Except for us.

32

Kicking the Wrong Cat

While we were living in the middle house in Emma Field, all the children slept in one room.

My bed was near the back wall, on the southwest side of the house.

We had several cats. Sometimes one, in particular, would get into the kitchen and make its way into our room. I would sometimes wake in the morning feeling a weight on my feet. It would be that cat lying on top of the cover over my feet.

I hated that. When I felt it I would draw back and kick the spot. That usually got rid of that cat for the moment.

Our beds were in a big room next to the kitchen and dining room to the north and next to a hall to the east which separated our room from the living room.

The only fireplace was in the living room. The wood burning cook stove was in the kitchen. The fire in the cook stove burned out early.

The fire in the living room stopped burning when we went to bed.

As a result there was no heat in the house for most of the night. The walls of the house were plain planks. To prevent the air from blowing in, small slats—thin boards—were nailed over the cracks between the planks. These were on the outside. That was the only shielding or insulation we had.

As the house grew older, more and more of these thin slats came loose and fell off and we did not always get them repaired very quickly.

One night during the early morning hours, a snowstorm came in from the southwest. There was little or no noise. It did not wake me up.

But one slat was missing. As a consequence snow blew in, landing on my bed. It was a thin pile, of course, but it was stacked up for inches.

I woke up about daylight. I felt a heavy weight on my feet.

"That cat," I thought.

I kicked. I really kicked hard.

And suddenly my face was covered with cold, chilling powder. It was snow, not a cat.

I got up and lit a lamp and found the answer. I quit kicking cats in the dark.

33

A Genuine Feud

So far as I know none of my kin folks ever engaged in a feud. But I heard some of the grown-ups talk about a feud that went on a long time but apparently had ended.

It took place in the lower end (or southwestern end) of Swain County and partly in Graham County.

From the best I could gather, the last person shot and killed in that feud was killed about five years before I was born.

The last man killed had killed the father of the man who later killed him. He was then tried and convicted of murder and went to prison for a term of years.

He was released from prison. The word got back to the community where he lived. That was Eagle Creek, located west of Hazel Creek and north of the Tennessee River.

The only son of his victim also lived on Eagle Creek.

He got word that his father's killer was getting out of prison and was on his way home.

That young man was then eighteen years of age.

He had no living brothers or sisters.

He loaded his rifle and found a place to lie in wait.

His target came. He was driving a one horse wagon and was sitting on a seat built onto the wagon bed. He had a loaded rifle laying across his knees.

He drove around a curve in the one track dirt road. The curve was necessary because a large rock lay above the road. His enemy was behind that rock.

As he drove into view a rifle fired. One shot and he was dead. He was the last person killed in that feud.

Law officers found his killer. He was tried, convicted and sent to prison for eight years.

He built his time and returned at twenty six years of age. In a few years he married and he and his wife had a son born to them.

It was not long after that when I met him. It was on Decoration Day and I saw him at the Watkins Graveyard.

Dad told me who he was and took me over and introduced me to him. I was very interested in learning what had happened.

He told me. And he told me in what appeared to be a frank and honest manner.

He didn't deny that he killed the man. He didn't deny that he hid and ambushed him.

He hadn't denied any of that in court.

What he said was that it was his duty to kill the man who had killed his father.

He offered no other explanation. I left him with a little better understanding of what moves some people in these mountains.

34

All White Feathers

I didn't know it when I was five years old. But I later learned that "to show the white feather" is a phrase from cockfighting and that a white feather in the tail of a gamecock is a sign of degenerate stock, not a true game-bird.

Dad traded in about everything: guns and knives and watches; horses and cattle and dogs; saws and hammers and axes. He even obtained a branded western cow at a sale in Bryson City one time. The cattle had just been hauled in by train.

And once he obtained one automobile in a trade but he didn't keep it long. He never learned to drive and he was no mechanic.

But he was good at sharpening axes and filing saws. He was also good as a blacksmith, a barber and a cobbler. He mended all our shoes and cut our hair. He cut our neighbors' hair and didn't charge for it.

And he was an expert on all breeds of hunting dogs.

But he never dealt in trading gamecocks. And he never really took part in cock fights or bet on any such fight.

But he did allow his friends to come to our place and to engage in what we called rooster fighting. That was usually on a Saturday afternoon in good weather.

That activity took place in a field above our barn.

There would be twelve or fifteen other men present and all carried their game roosters to the place and all carried a pair of "steels" to place over the rooster's natural spurs which would act in much the same way as a dagger.

The steel was hollow in a place to fit over the natural spur and shaft on the end. It had leather strings attached to it to tie around the rooster's legs to hold the steels on.

Among Dad's many friends who came was Will Howell, then over eighty years old. He was one of about four black men, as we called them, who came regularly. And all of them also went fox hunting with Dad on other occasions.

Times were tough. It was hard to make money.

But all the rooster owners bet on their champions.

One Saturday afternoon, Will Howell brought a white game rooster with him. None of us had seen it before.

When it came his time to match his champion, Mr. Howell already had the spurs on the rooster. He bet a dollar against another rooster. Both owners set down their champions.

The other rooster facing Mr. Howell's white rooster hopped up and crowed.

That was usual and routine.

We expected the white rooster to follow suit.

But he didn't. He ducked his head. Then he turned and ran. Away from his opponent. He headed toward the barn.

Mr. Howell didn't hesitate. He took off after that white rooster.

For an old man he ran fast. In fact, he amazed us all. He caught that rooster and grabbed him.

We were all watching.

Mr. Howell stopped. Then he grabbed that rooster's head in his right hand and he "wrung" that rooster's neck, throwing it down dead as a doornail.

We all heard him say: "If ye won't fight, durn ye, I'm through with ye."

He paused. Then he reached down and picked up the rooster again and removed the two steels, placing them in his hip pocket.

He left the dead rooster there. Nothing else was said.

But he did pay off the dollar bet to the other owner.

35

A Revival and Its Side Effects

Mom was a devout church member. All the people I knew were Baptist and, over the years, we attended three different Baptist churches: Franklin Grove Baptist Church, Rock Creek Baptist Church and Spruce Grove Baptist Church.

One of Mom's uncles, John Medlin, was a Baptist preacher. Her grandfather, Marion Medlin, was a Baptist preacher. Her brother, Jud Medlin, was a Baptist preacher. Her brother, Charles Medlin, was a Baptist preacher. Dad's brother-in-law, Uncle Rob Branton, was a Baptist preacher.

And we had many friends of the family who were Baptist preachers.

Revival meetings were carried on at the churches we knew. These were usually held in late summer, after the crops were laid by but before all the harvesting was done.

One of our uncles was carrying on a revival with another Baptist preacher. Our whole family attended each night.

But each night, before Church began, our uncle and his associate came to our house and ate supper.

We didn't usually serve chicken for supper. But on these occasions we did—every night.

The number of our chickens was limited, to my knowledge.

And I embarrassed Mom terribly with that knowledge.

The Revival had been on for each night, Sunday through Wednesday and on Thursday evening we were having chicken for supper again. The two preachers were at the dining table as was Mom and all us children.

Dad was away in a logging camp.

We had about finished eating when I asked my uncle's associate how long the revival would last.

He said he just didn't know.

I turned to my brother, Walt, and I said: "Walt, if we don't hurry up and git this over with, we're going to run out of chicken."

No one else said anything.

Later, when Dad got home, I overheard Mom explaining to him how embarrassed she was by my remark.

But I also took note that the revival ended on that Thursday night.

36

A Standing Dead Mule

Dad loved humor. He was a practical joker. He would go to great lengths to play pranks on us children and on his friends.

One of the most elaborate shows I ever witnessed was with Mr. Will Howell who fox hunted with Dad.

Mr. Howell had a pure bred Walker fox hound. It had the usual white and orange color, the fast feet, the sharp nose and the tail curved up over its back.

Dad really wanted to own that dog. And he made all kinds of offers for it. But no trade developed.

Dad would trade one horse or mule or cow for an older one and get boot in the trade—five or ten dollars in cash. Sometimes he got even more boot than that .

But as he kept on trading and making boot on each trade, he obtained a horse or mule or cow harder to trade next time.

He did that in one series of trades and wound up with a mule at least thirty years old, one that had no teeth and very little strength.

That mule couldn't eat corn, even if you shelled it for him.

Walt and I had to make mush for that mule to eat, mixing corn meal with water, stirring it up and giving it to the mule in a bucket.

And we got no work out of that mule. We did the work in feeding and watering it and that was that.

The weather grew cold.

One very cold, frosty morning I went to the barn to check about feeding the mule.

He was placed in a stable at night. He was in the stable, but he was lying down, a highly unusual thing.

I went in to the mule and spoke. He didn't move. He was on one side, his legs sticking out and his head on the ground.

I touched him. He was cold as ice and he didn't move.

I ran to the house and told Dad.

Dad and I and Walt walked back to the barn. Dad took one look and said that the mule was dead and frozen stiff. He said we'd have to hitch a steer to him and pull him out of the stall and bury him.

It wasn't getting any warmer and it was very uncomfortable doing that kind of work.

But Walt and I tied a heavy rope around the mule and hitched up the steer and pulled the mule out of the stall. Dad stopped us.

"I jist thought of somethin," he said. "Let's pull 'im around to the front side of the barn and stand 'im up."

We did just that.

It was a tough job, but we got him on his four feet, his body leaning against the barn and facing the trail to the barn. He was also on the side of the barn where the sun would hit him.

Then Dad let us in on why he did that.

He told Walt to go to town, where Will Howell lived, and to tell Will Howell that he would swap him a mule for that Walker fox hound and to bring that hound on over there that morning.

Walt left. He was gone more than two hours. Then he appeared with Mr. Howell leading that Walker fox hound. They stopped in the yard at our house.

Dad and I joined them. The mule was still standing. And the sun was shining on it.

The barn was about two hundred feet away from our house. From our yard the mule could be seen but not well seen.

Dad offered the trade. Mr. Howell said "Yes" and handed to Dad the dog chain holding the hound. Dad tied the chain to a porch post and, leaving the dog there, we all started walking toward the barn. Walt and I walked behind the two men.

I wish I could remember precisely every word of the conversation Walt and I heard as we followed Dad and Mr. Howell to the barn.

Mr. Howell had questions and Dad answered all the questions and didn't lie by any of his answers. He also didn't give out much information by his answers.

The questions and answers went somewhat like this.

"Is that mule broke to work?"

"Oh yes, he's been trained to work a long time."

"Is that a mean mule?"

"Ah! No! That mule is about the tamest mule you ever saw."

"Will that mule kick you?"

"No, I guarantee that mule will never take a kick at anyone."

We were up close by now and Mr. Howell walked up in front of the mule.

His next question was: "Can that mule see?" The answer was: "He can see as well right now as he could this mornin'."

With that, Mr. Howell put his hand up in front of the mule's eyes and moved his hand up and down.

"Why! That mule cain't see a durn thing," he said.

"Yeah," Dad said, almost bursting to laugh. "Why don't you feel of his ears?"

Mr. Howell did. Then he said: "That mule is as dead as a door knob."

"Yeah," Dad said. "You jist go back down there and take your dog home."

We all laughed big and loud and long.

Mr. Howell took his dog back home.

But in a few days he traded that dog to Dad but not for a mule—dead or alive.

37

To Carry a Cat

I don't wish to gripe about the way I was brought up but, upon reflection, it seems to me that I had to learn a lot of things the hard way.

Upon further reflection, I believe that much of that happened because I didn't ask the right questions ahead of time.

But how many children not yet in school would ask an older person how to carry a tom cat?

We had one cow. So did most families. The family cow provided the family with milk. But when that cow went dry for a while, we had to borrow milk elsewhere. Mom usually borrowed milk from her mother.

Mom sent me over the hill to carry back home a gallon of milk in a bucket from Gram Ma Medlin's.

When I got there Gram Ma Medlin asked me to carry a cat home to Mom which Gram Ma Medlin was giving to her.

I placed the cat under my right arm, holding it under its chest with my hand. I took the gallon bucket of milk in my left hand and started walking home. I made it fine about half way home. Then the cat started trying to get loose. I set the bucket down on the ground so I could use both hands to hold the cat and to calm it down a bit. But that cat got almost entirely free. All I could do was to grab it by the tail with my right hand.

That was a mistake. That cat went all over me. It scratched me in places I didn't even know I had. I looked like a war victim.

But finally I was able to get it by the back of the neck with my right hand. That worked. That way I held it.

I got the bucket and I carried the cat on by the neck.

After that, I knew how to carry a cat.

Or, perhaps, more accurately, I knew how not to carry a cat.

38

The Borrowed Champion

The second enterprise Walt and I got into that summer was a little more risky. But like most risky ventures it seemed to have more potential.

By being careful we accumulated enough money to buy nine Banty pullets. We got two young Banty roosters, too, but they didn't last long. They were a big part of that risk I just mentioned.

The two roosters did well in growing up. It was at that point where they started reaching maturity that the trouble started. Crowing was what did it.

I don't mean a full-out, mature, confident, devil-may-care, challenging crow. They never got that far, which is indeed the saddest part of all. If one must be cut down so young, it seemed to me that at least he ought to have had a chance to throw out some significant challenge before it all ended for him. The two great things in my life right then, though only vaguely recognized as such by me, were my home — the Great Smokies, and the economic situation—the Great Depression. I could mount very little challenge to either; so I guess what I did was to let them challenge each other while I gave my attention to lesser things.

My Gram Ma was awful fond of saying that "a whistlin' girl and a crowin' hen always come to some bad end." Yet I never heard her say anything so prophetic about a crowing rooster. 'Course I've noticed, myself, that when a man r'ares back and starts into crowing, something bad is usually about to happen.

Still, crowing is a rooster's nature. And those two took to it like a duck takes to water.

The first one started on a Sunday morning, but not early, at dawn, which is the usual case. It was about mid morning. No doubt he had been listening to Uncle Lum's old Dominecker rooster.

Uncle Lum lived up the hollow from us. He had bought a part of Gram Pa's old place and built a house above our spring. I never did think that was very neighborly. Dad never said so, but I think he agreed with me. Mom didn't say anything, either; Uncle Lum was her cousin, but since he was older than Mom, all of us called him Uncle. Back then, older people were uncle or aunt whether related or not.

He kept a cow and usually a hog. He had a rogue steer, too, and a whole flock of chickens. He always had several dogs around but they were never any good, not even worth their feed, Dad figured. And nobody knew any more about dogs or horses or cows than Dad.

Most of Uncle Lum's chickens were not much, either; still, he did have that one big old Dominecker rooster.

He was a big scutter, and mean. He was twice the size of an ordinary Dominecker, three times as big as a Game rooster and maybe five times the size of a full grown Banty rooster. He had spurs about an inch and a half long. Sharp and ugly they were. He knew how to use them and for what. It was pure delight for him to show off his spurs around the hens. He would circle them from left to right, clucking, chuckling, chortling and stopping now and then to kick leaves or grass backwards, first with one foot and then with the other. The spurs would flash and the hens would peck and go "Cluck uh, cluck uh, cluck uh loo."

The ultimate show off to him was to find a new rooster, always smaller than he and usually quite young and brash, just then feeling the throaty ecstasy of a good crow.

That is the way he found our two Banty roosters.

The first one went on that Sunday. He hadn't really gotten up a good crow yet, and his first feeble efforts died in his throat. He tried a few more calls and finally got up enough wind and sound for the young Banty hens to notice. The other Banty rooster, not yet advanced enough to give rise to a crow, looked on with curiosity and some envy, it seemed. But his envy, like most envy, was sorely misplaced. For up the road the Old Dominecker heard those first feeble imagined threats to his domain.

To him this was heresy. It ran counter to the established word—

that he was the Cock of the Roost, the Proud Overseer of all he surveyed, the Lord Protector of the Hens, the Progenitor and Guardian of all feathered fowl, the King, the Eternal Conqueror.

He moved with dispatch to protect his image and to quell this young upstart who would dare foment disruption to the Kingdom. For that could confuse the hens, distract the pullets, create general unrest and even lead the young biddies into ways foreign to the accepted sovereignty.

I heard him coming, those big, heavy feet sounding "Pat, Pat, Pat" on the dirt road, his hoarse, guttural clucking displaying immense displeasure toward the young upstart but also revealing his blood-thirsty zest for the encounter.

He rounded the curve, passing the big black walnut tree and the last Early Harvest apple tree. On he came, with one purpose propelling him forward: destroy the heretic!

The little Banty never dreamed of the impending danger. Like most young idealists, he was curious only about his own ideas at the moment. He saw no general confusion among the hens. His aim was not to entice away the pullets. He wasn't even thinking of the biddies. He was merely trying to get that "crow" straightened out, to get it in tune so that it would stop vibrating up and down, first fine and then coarse, and really not coming out with any uniformity at all.

He was in the middle of a new trial run when calamity struck. And, as I saw it, it was not only an unfair encounter but the Old Dominecker didn't even give fair notice. There was no "On guard" or "Fore" or "Hey, I'm coming" call or anything like that. He simply bowled over the young one, bulldozed him and put the spurs to the victim. In a second it was over. Those spurs struck so swiftly the human eye could hardly follow. The onward rush of the Old Dominecker was not even slowed. And when he passed on, the young one had tried his last crow.

The Old Dominecker circled, chortling to himself again, pulling down his left wing to drag the ground as he circled, with the down wing on the inside of the circle. Midway the circle he stopped, peered sharply at the fallen heretic, scratched first with one foot, then the other, kicking each foot high to the back. Then he rared way back and crowed. It was his signal of victory. Once again the Kingdom was safe.

Well, the second Banty rooster went the same way, about a week later.

The significance of the blood purge on the previous Sunday was entirely lost on him. Or perhaps he understood that bloody Sunday and just didn't care that much. If so, his idealism was tragic. For he was the last rooster our Banty hens had. Oh, of course, Old Dominecker would have been glad to oblige. But he would have had to reckon with outside interference, namely, me and Walt. That kind of thing is sometimes justified. At least, that was my view of that situation.

We took counsel, Walt and I. The only rooster left in the hollow was Old Dominecker. He had disposed of Dad's last big rooster a couple of weeks before he hit our first Banty. The big hens were still laying, but there was a foreseeable end to that. That is, unless we adopted Old Dominecker's views. And somehow his charm had not gotten through to me the same way it had to his captive audience of non-voting hens that kept house up at Uncle Lum's place. And our Banty hens had not started laying yet.

Walt and I decided we would just have to help nature along and persuade those Banty pullets, just now coming to maturity, to take over a setting of big hen eggs. Banties are great setters. They are still close enough to the wild to be good parents. And they will set on big chicken eggs just as well, adopting those that hatch as their own, whether they are as big as Rhode Island Reds or Barred Plymouth Rocks or even turkeys, I guess. They'll raise 'em, clucking and mothering and scratching for their adopted children even up to the time when the young ones are towering over them and ought to be out doing their own scratching.

Game chickens are the same way, only more so, for they are closer to the wild than even the Banties. They are still good fliers, better than Banties; although a Banty can still get up a good flight. They are magnificent from a hill top or a high tree.

Big chickens are grounded. Most of them won't even try to fly. And occasionally when one does, he is awkward at it, taking about an hour and a hundred yard dash to get off the ground, then wallowing around in the air a few feet off the ground, wobbling first this way and then that, and finally hitting the ground like a dodo, after a fifteen or twenty yard flight. A seasoned chicken-killing dog will usually catch one on the ground, but if one should take to the air, he can sometimes get it with a good running jump or, if that fails, outrun it and gobble it up as it comes to a tumbling, flopping landing.

Walt and I got to talking about that about a week after our last rooster bit the dust. We went from big chickens to Banties to Games.

Walt said, "I wish we had a Game rooster with spurs as long as that Old Dominecker has."

"There ain't any such rooster in the world," I said, in a way that would ordinarily stop that line of talk.

"Well, you know, they use steels on Games," Walt said, opening up a whole new line of thought.

"Yeah," I said, "Dad has a pair of steels in his old tool box. I saw him put 'um on that Game rooster when they had the chicken fights last fall up there at the barn."

"Let's get 'um," Walt said, getting up ready to go to the tool box.

"Well, we ain't got no rooster to put 'um on," I argued, "and I couldn't do much good with them on me. I'd ruther jest stomp Old Dominecker and be done with it."

"Dad'd whup you good with his razor strop if you stomped 'im," Walt said. "No, we've got to have a fair fight and kill 'im that way."

"You cain't do it with a hen, and you ain't got no rooster," I said, still thinking I had a good logical argument there.

"We could borrie one," Walt said. I looked at him hard, then; I had never heard of anybody borrowing a rooster. Usually you borrowed salt, or maybe sugar or coffee, but you didn't borrow a man's gun or his dog — let alone his rooster. Why, that would be worse than trying to borrow a man's cow!

I didn't think that was exactly what Sampson meant when he told the Philistines that they could not have solved his riddle if they had not been plowing with his heifer.

I had been reading a book which I got from the library over in town telling about how in England, in the old days, they hired Champions to fight a battle called "Trial by Battle" when these people got into lawsuits over land or kidnapped wives or that sort of thing. But hiring a Champion was not quite the same as borrowing one. And I had heard the older folks talk about how the railroad and the lumber companies hired lawyers to fight in Court for them. But they never had mentioned "borrowing" a lawyer. It was to be a long time before I ran into anything approaching that, like a legislative lobbyist or an "amicus curiae" brief.

"I never heard of such a thing," I said, thinking that that ended the discussion. "And, besides," I put in, with a thought that just occurred to me, "Where would you borrie one, anyhow?"

"I bet Glenn James would let us have one," Walt said, heading for the tool box again.

I didn't answer. I sat there and thought about it. I could hear Walt fumbling around in Dad's tool box.

It was true. Glenn James had a whole bunch of fighting Games. I had learned most of what I knew about Game chickens from watching Glenn's, with a little closer knowledge of the way they actually fought with steel on by watching a few prize fights with Walt when Dad and the other men didn't know we were peeking.

Glenn lived down on that big creek. His Game chickens nested all over the hillsides and in the woods. I had helped him find their nests by watching a hen rise and fly from a grove of trees or a hillside, then back tracking her and usually going fifteen or twenty yards further in. I had become pretty good at it and Glenn was always grateful. I figured he was a pretty good friend and might — just might — go along with the idea.

I was still pondering it when Walt came back. He had found the steels and had them in his hand. They were bright and shiny, and very dangerous when you tried to tie them on the legs of a good Game rooster.

"The strops are in good shape," Walt said, holding them out for me to see. "And the steels are as sharp as a pin."

I looked and nodded agreement.

"Let's go to Glenn's," he said then.

"What are you going to tell 'im?" I asked. "You cain't tell 'im you want to borrie his rooster to fight Old Dominecker. Besides, you may get his rooster killed. Then what would you do?"

"We'll get the best one he's got. And he will shore kill Old Dominecker if we put the steels on him. We'll jist tell Glenn we don't have a rooster and we need one with our hens. And that's so." I couldn't argue with that last part. I got up to go with him.

"You better put the steels back," I said.

"No," Walt answered, "I'll hide 'um in the corn crib so they'll be handy."

He headed for the corn crib and I waited.

It didn't take him long to hide them. He came back, walking fast and grinning. We left for Glenn's. We didn't announce to anyone where we were going. On the way we talked it over some more but it always came out just like Walt had said it at first.

Glenn was home and came out when we called. He asked about Mom and Dad and Gram Pa and Gram Ma and the younger children.

"Everybody's fine," we said.

"Found any more nests?" I asked, opening up to get to the main question. "Yeah, one or two," he said. "Some of 'um are still hidin' out, though. I'll have to get you to help me Saturday and we'll find 'um all."

"All right with me," I answered, and stopped there.

"How's yore Banties?" he asked. He knew about our latest enterprise.

Walt cut in at that. "The hens are fine," he said. "But that Old Dominecker of Uncle Lum's killed our last rooster." He rushed right on into it. "We thought we might borrie a Game rooster from you for a little while."

Glenn looked at Walt and then at me. Neither of us said anything more.

"Why, yeah. I guess we could do that. I like mixed chickens purty good myself. I've got a Blue out here in the coop. He's purty wild and a dern good fighter. But if you keep 'im in a coop a while 'til he gits used to the place and the hens, I guess he'd stay all right."

I couldn't keep from grinning. This was real luck. A fighter was what we came for.

Glenn got him out. He was pretty. And big, too, with shiny tail feathers and a big red comb.

I looked at his legs. He didn't have spurs like Old Dominecker's, just nubs where his spurs had been filed off to fix them where the steels would fit. I was glad we'd found the steels in the tool box. "We'll take good care of 'im," Walt said. "And we won't need 'im long."

I wished he'd shut up. We knew what we planned and it wouldn't take very long for that—one way or the other—but I didn't know how long it would take to get some mixed chickens. But Glenn didn't perk up at that.

"Take your time, boys," he said. "I'll let you know when I need 'im."

As we left, I wondered why he didn't inquire further about Old Dominecker. We had told him what had happened to our roosters.

And here we were taking his Blue into danger and him with no spurs, just nubs. And Glenn didn't know about the steels we'd found. Even if he wasn't worried, I wondered if I ought to be.

It was getting dark when we got home. That was a good thing, for the chickens were going to roost and usually roosters don't crow that late. If there had been another rooster around, the Game would have crowed even that late in spite of the Dickens. We slipped in and I told Walt to hold him by the throat until we got him in a coop. That way he could choke off a crow and maybe discourage that sort of thing. We weren't ready to take on Old Dominecker and, besides, I didn't want any of the folks to know too much about our business at that point.

We lucked out again. We got the Blue in the coop and got corn and water to him without a crow and with none of the folks being any the wiser.

We left him and went to supper. Right after that we went to bed. Sunrise came early and I knew what would happen next morning. Old Dominecker thought he had to wake the whole world up and I knew the Blue would be answering. Before that happened we had to have him out, walking free, with a pair of good steel spurs on.

That night I dreamed of looking for hens' nests at Glenn's place. Every time I found a nest of eggs I could hear a rooster crow. Each time it had that guttural, hoarse sound of Old Dominecker. And then I could see Old Dominecker bowling over that Banty rooster, chortling and chuckling and circling to the left, his wing down, comb up and eyes peering. I woke up a couple of times and it was hard to go back to sleep.

Just before dawn I woke up again. I punched Walt and he woke. We listened for the clock and in a minute or two it struck five. The time had come. We eased out of bed, put our pants on and slid barefooted out the back door.

We raced past the barn to the coop. The Blue was still there and he cackled a bit, but he didn't crow. Walt had some trouble getting his hands through the slats and laying hold of both legs. He finally made it and I lifted the side of the coop and Walt pulled him out.

We didn't have the steels. Walt handed the Blue to me and ran to the corn crib. I held him under my arm with both his feet in my right hand and my left hand on his throat. As Walt came back I had to choke off one crow the Blue had started.

"Hold his legs out, one at a time," Walt said. "I'll tie these on."

The Blue cocked his head on one side and, as Walt laid one steel on the ground, he arched his neck. He tried to crow again and I made a grab at his throat. I had some trouble but I stopped it.

"Don't let 'im crow yit. We ain't ready," Walt said.

"I got 'im now," I said, and gingerly pushed out one leg.

Walt did a splendid job, fast, and straight to the point. The Blue held still until the first steel was tied firmly. Then Walt had to help me hold that leg for a few seconds, for the Blue was struggling to get loose. He'd arch his neck and squirm and try to crow. I guess he knew something was up. And it wasn't easy, holding his throat with one hand and trying to hold two legs apart, one with a razor sharp steel tied on, and me with only two hands to do it all.

He settled down then and Walt went to work on the other steel.

In about three seconds he said, "O.K. Give 'im to me. I've got 'um."

I obliged, easy as I could. Walt got him under his arm, with his right hand holding the legs, and his left holding him gently under the throat.

We had to go by the house. It was not quite light yet, and nobody else was up.

The dew was heavy on the grass and a little fog was circling the hill tops. The stars were fading out. We walked by the house, easy, and on bare feet we didn't make a sound. Dad's dogs didn't take notice. They were used to us.

We passed the chimney corner and headed for the curve of the road, where the black walnut and the Early Harvest trees stood.

Our timing could not have been better. We hadn't quite reached the curve and had slowed down when I heard a Jo Ree start his chirping in the laurels across the meadow. "Jo Ree! Joe Ree! Joe Ree!" I knew he was hopping from one limb to the next after each "Jo Ree."

"Wait, Walt," I said. "It's about time for Old Dominecker to start." Walt stopped. The Blue arched his neck and started pecking the air. He struggled to get loose. Walt held on.

It was getting lighter. I heard the Jo Ree again. And then I saw a jay bird fly to the top of the Early Harvest. He wasn't saying anything, which was unusual for him. Maybe he was waiting for someone else to wake up the world.

And then it came. From the big holly above our spring came that gutteral, hoarse, bugle call. It sounded louder than I had ever heard it. It went all up and down the hollow. And I could hear it echo back from the hillsides. It came again, this time loud and clear and long. Old Dominecker was awake and reasserting his Lordship of the Universe.

Walt was having trouble. The Blue was really struggling now to get loose. Walt was holding on tight and about to choke him with his left hand.

Even so, the Blue was close to getting loose.

"Slack off on his throat, Walt, Let 'im crow."

Walt slacked off. The Blue arched his neck and r'ared back. He crowed. Long and loud and clear. I never heard better. It was almost deafening. He crowed again, longer and louder this time. Oh, it was magnificent. Old Dominecker never crowed louder than that!

Then Old Dominecker answered. This time it was an angry call, lower and throatier and with more force in it. The Blue crowed for the third time. Then he started trying to get loose again. Walt asked me to help hold him and as I got both hands on him, we slowly lowered him to the ground, with Walt hanging on to those two legs. Just as we got his feet settled on the ground, and still holding on, Old Dominecker flew out of the holly heading our way.

"Let's turn 'im loose, Walt."

It was about time for the Blue was about to get loose from both of us. He had seen his antagonist fly toward the ground and must have known he was headed his way.

"O.K. Let'er rip," Walt answered, and we both turned loose and backed off.

The Blue didn't rush forward right away like I thought he would. He minced around a few steps, going nowhere and walking wide to keep his steels apart. Then he stopped and arched his neck, looking ahead. He lowered his head to the ground, raised it again and shook himself. Again he arched his neck and the neck feathers stood up, wide apart and ruffled all along.

He crowed again, getting his full body into it.

When he stopped and the echo faded, I heard Old Dominecker answer, crowing as he ran our way, the crow starting and stopping, going up and down as he bounced along on the ground. He was coming by the spring trail. I heard him chuckling and chortling and then I could hear those big feet going "Pat, Pat, Pat."

The Blue still hadn't gone forward. He stood there, his feet wide apart, planted firmly; his head was high and moving in short jabs, downward and up, first to the right and then to the left. Then he got still, his head high, listening, looking.

Old Dominecker topped the rise, coming into sight at a full gallop, about thirty feet away and even with the black walnut. He came on at full speed. I remembered how he had run over the Banty like a freight train. I thought he would do it that way again.

"Let's move back, Walt."

But then I hushed. The Blue cackled, not a crow, just one dry cackle. And then he moved; slowly he took two steps forward, stepping wide, looking, and stopped. Old Dominecker was about fifteen feet away. The cackle and the movement had its effect. He put on his brakes, hard. He skidded and almost sat down. But he stopped - about ten feet away from the Blue. The Blue cackled again. Old Dominecker had quit chuckling. He just stared.

The Blue cackled again, and slowly lowered his head toward the ground. Those neck feathers all stood up again, arched and ruffled. He scratched twice, faster this time.

Old Dominecker followed suit. His big head went toward the ground, the neck feathers spread out.

The Blue crowed. Old Dominecker answered.

Then each started forward, mincing, wary, on guard. They inched forward and then both stopped. They were still about six feet apart. Then each circled a little, each going a little to his left. About four feet separated them. Again each lowered his head to the ground.

It was daylight now. The jay bird was sounding off. And I heard a red bird in one of the apple trees.

But Old Dominecker and the Blue were oblivious to that. I heard a cow bawl, but they took no notice.

They circled some more and got within about two feet of each other. The Blue had now made a quarter circle and held the upper ground on the high side of the road. Old Dominecker had kept pace on the circle. Walt and I were standing mighty still, hardly breathing, absorbed in the drama.

Then the Blue moved. Suddenly he went straight up in the air, about two feet off the ground, his wings flapping a little, and his feet forward, pedaling, bicycle like, whirring, so fast you could hardly see, but with the steels flashing by each other, with very little passing room, but enough, not hitting each other or getting in the way. He had tested them; everything was in order. He came back to the ground, steady on his feet, watching, waiting. Old Dominecker tried the same thing, only he didn't get more than half as high, for he was a great deal bigger and heavier. I saw those long spurs whirring but I didn't think they were as fast as the Blue's. And he wound up differently. He didn't come back to the ground stopping and steady like the Blue. He hit coming forward, that freight train on the tracks, headed for the kill. It looked for an instance like Bloody Sunday all over again, when he had bowled over the Banty.

Just before he reached the Blue he went into the air again, those long spurs forward and whirring, his big body carried forward by the momentum, hitting the exact spot where the Blue stood.

But the Blue was no longer there. He was in the air, too, steels flashing forward. He was far above Old Dominecker and just before the bigger one hit the ground, those steels struck, both of them. They both caught the head of Old Dominecker, one on each side and both flashed in. The right stuck until Old Dominecker hit the ground, and then pulled out. The left one stayed, buried deep.

The Blue hit the ground on his right foot and jerked his left to free it. It stayed and the Blue circled on the one foot, dragging the bigger rooster. About a quarter circle and he stopped, peered and listened. I could hear a rattle, faint, in the throat of Old Dominecker. The Blue heard it too. He crowed.

Then he circled some more, about a quarter circle and he stopped and crowed again.

The right steel was dripping blood, the left was still stuck and Old Dominecker was a dead weight now.

"Let's catch 'im, Hub," Walt said, "he's killed the old rascal."

It was over. It had seemed a long time. I thought surely it had to be about noon. But the fog hadn't lifted a foot on the hills since it all started. And the jay bird was still there, only quiet now. The Jo Ree was still hopping in the same laurel. I heard that cow bawl again.

We both grabbed the Blue. He was hard to hold, but we pushed him to the ground and Walt got the right steel off. He then unstrapped the left one and freed the Blue's other leg, and jerked the steel out.

"Let 'im go," he said. "We'll catch him later on." I did as he said.

Old Dominecker was dead. There was no doubt about that. And the Blue had gone off about twenty feet and crowed again.

"What'll we do?" I asked. "That crowing will wake Dad up."

"I'll throw 'im up here on the bank" said Walt, as he picked up Old Dominecker and laid him on the bank on the upper side of the road. "I'd better wash these steels off and put 'um back."

We headed for the branch. Walt washed off the steels and dried them on his pants legs. Back to the house and the tool box we went and Walt got the steels back in.

Nobody else was up. We went back outside. "What'll we do?" I asked again.

"Well, we'll have to tell Dad exactly what happened."

"Gosh," I said. I couldn't think of anything else.

We told Dad after breakfast. And we took him and showed him the dead rooster. He spotted the Blue, too, and looked him over from a distance.

"You boys shouldn't have done that," he said, but he didn't mention the razor strop, which was encouraging. "You'll have to go tell Uncle Lum. And you'll probably have to pay him for his rooster."

He walked back to the house, leaving me and Walt and the dead rooster on the bank.

"Good gosh, Walt, if we have to pay fer 'im, why didn't we just buy 'im and chop his head off with the axe."

"No," Walt said, "that wouldn't do. We had to get 'im in a fair fight. Choppin' his head off wouldn't have been fair ner half as much fun. And, besides, he wouldn't 'uv sold 'im to us, anyhow."

I puzzled on that, but I didn't argue. After all Walt, at nine, was two years older and knew more about such things. I guess you had to learn about being fair as you got older. And though he hadn't put it quite that way, I guess he was right about not buying the old rascal. Even if Uncle Lum would have sold him, we couldn't have bought him because we didn't have anything to buy with.

That thought struck me and I said, "What if he makes us pay fer 'im? We're so pore now we couldn't buy a rooster and had to go borrie one."

"We'll see." And the older brother had the last word again, like he was supposed to.

We started up to Uncle Lum's house. We walked slowly. About

halfway there I stopped and said to Walt: "I bet they're not even up yit. That cow is still bawling, so nobody's milked her yet."

"Yeah, they are. I see smoke from the stove pipe." That meant somebody was cooking breakfast on the wood stove.

"All right. We might as well do it now," I muttered, not feeling at all good about it.

We called Uncle Lum out. Walt told him our rooster had killed his rooster. "Huh, huh, huh," he laughed, sounding awful much like Old Dominecker chortling, it seemed to me. "You boys must have the wrong rooster. Your rooster might have killed somebody else's, but it didn't kill mine. Mine is big and has big long spurs and is a real fighter. You must be sorta mixed up."

"Well, you can come and see fer yoreself," Walt answered.

"I'll come and look, but it couldn't be mine," replied Uncle Lum, and we started back down the road.

When we got there and looked on the bank, Uncle Lum's eyes almost popped out.

"Well, I do believe that's my rooster," he said a little quizzically, but not laughing anymore, now. "What kind of rooster have you boys got?"

"That's 'im over yonder," Walt said, pointing over toward the Blue standing in the edge of the cane field. "We got 'im from Glenn James."

"Why, that's a Game," said Uncle Lum. "You didn't tell me you had a Game rooster. You boys oughta told me so I could'a put mine up."

"We didn't git 'im 'till last night," Walt explained.

"Yeah, yore Old Dominecker was probi'ly already gone to roost," I put in. "And we didn't have much time this mornin'." I left out that part about having the Blue in the coop that morning but then I wasn't buying that business about putting that Old Dominecker up anyhow. He hadn't put him up to keep him off our place and off our Banty roosters. And he knew about his rooster cleaning us plumb out of roosters. So I didn't feel too bad about leaving out that part about the coop.

"Well, you boys'll just have to pay me fer 'im," he said, as he took hold of both legs of the dead rooster and picked him up, holding him down, with his head dragging the ground.

About then he spotted Dad, who had come back out on the front porch.

"Ervin," he yelled, "yore boys' Game rooster has done killed my little rooster." I marveled at how that old rooster had gone from "big" with "big long spurs" to "little" in so short a time. The way I saw it any man who could change things around that fast, if he started at it young, could make a pretty fair lawyer of himself or most certainly a leading member of the state legislature.

Dad called back: "Yeah, the boys told me about it and I sent 'um up to tell ye."

"Oh, I see," said Uncle Lum, as if that were complete news to him. "Well, I could have got a dollar and a half fer 'im. I think they ought to pay me."

"I told them to work that out with ye," Dad called.

"Oh, you did?" And again it sounded like that was news to him.

I couldn't help thinking that he had never offered to pay for our two roosters or Dad's either, for that matter. But neither Walt nor Dad was objecting to paying and they knew more about it than I did, I figured.

Uncle Lum turned back to me and Walt. "I'll have to have a dollar and a half, boys."

"We don't have it now, but we'll git it," Walt answered.

"All right. I'll be expecting it," and he slung the old rooster over his shoulder and headed for home.

After he disappeared around the curve I said to Walt: "Do you mean we have to give him a dollar and a half and don't even git to keep that old rooster?"

"That's right, Hub. Let 'im take 'im. He'll have to boil 'im fer a week and it will still be the toughest chewin' he has ever done."

That didn't explain it all, but it was good enough.

When Saturday morning came, Walt told Dad we were going to take the Blue home.

"You boys ketch 'im and I'll go with ye," Dad told us.

The Blue was pretty well used to the place by then and wasn't so wild. He had got well acquainted with all our hens and, being the only rooster in the hollow, had pretty well wedded Uncle Lum's flock to ours. At least I noticed that Uncle Lum's hens seemed to hang around our house more than they used to.

Walt got an ear of corn and shelled it and all the chickens flocked around. While the Blue was eating and not watching too well I got both hands on his legs. Walt helped to hold him and Dad tied his legs with a string. Walt carried him.

When we got to his house, Glenn was expecting me to help hunt nests. But he was a little surprised we brought the Blue home so soon. Dad told him about the steels and Uncle Lum's dead rooster. Glenn grinned real broad and didn't say anything.

"He's charging the boys a dollar and a half," Dad said. "And he took the old rooster home with him."

"Bet that'll be tough eatin'," allowed Glenn, still grinning big. "Say, Walt, why don't you help me and Hub hunt them nests today?"

Walt said that would be fine, Dad went on over to Peach Tree Creek to see somebody over there.

We hunted until about noon and found several full nests. Glenn must have had a half bushel of Game eggs by dinner time. He said he was going to set them all and maybe we could pick us out a young rooster when they hatched. That sounded fine to me.

"I shore want a Blue if ye git one," I said.

Glenn said that suited him and then added: "You boys have done a good job. Here is seventy-five a piece for you."

"Thanks," we both said together. I certainly hadn't expected any pay.

On the way home Walt said, "Well, we've got our dollar and a half between us. We'll pay off Uncle Lum this evenin'."

I hated to give it up so soon, but I figured I'd just be wasting my breath to argue it. Older people usually have their way about such matters, anyhow.

39

She "Tuck" a Through

In the Baptist Church which we attended for a long time—Franklin Grove Baptist Church—we had some of the finest citizens in Swain County as members. And we had good, sensible pastors. Sunday School was not only educational but also enjoyable.

Again—as with almost about everything I can remember—I wish I had asked more questions.

But I did learn and I did enjoy attending church.

We almost always had a sermon preached each Sunday night.

That was one of my favorites.

And perhaps for the wrong reason.

I went Sunday night for the entertainment. It didn't always happen but when it did, it was worth the walk there and back.

We had a member named Clementine. She had two sons. They always attended Sunday night service with Clementine and her husband.

Clementine was one of the very first members who would get "happy" during the sermon and "shout."

But she was in the choir and the choir sat up front, next to the pulpit.

While the preacher was preaching, Clementine would sometimes get up and "shout."

The shout in her case consisted in her rising to her feet, placing both feet firmly together, clapping her hands in front of her, shouting "Hooey" and jumping forward with stiff legs about six inches. That routine was repeated over and over.

But that wasn't all.

She always wore an apron over her dress as if she were going to be cooking or washing dishes.

And her youngest son would inevitably run after her, grab her apron strings behind her and follow her across the stage.

And also, inevitably, her husband would run after the son to try to catch him and take him off stage.

All the kids in the audience would stand up on the benches, or even sit on the top of the benches, better to see what was going on.

I'm sure it wouldn't match movies or TV of today but it was real entertainment for us.

And then, during the next week, I would sometimes hear some woman report what happened to some other woman member who was not present for the show.

In a shouting spell, the shouter usually goes through the crowd, and that is how those ladies would express it by saying: "Yeah, Clementine tuck (took) a through last night."

40

Directing Traffic—In Fits

D ad owned thirty-six dogs at one time. How he was able to feed them and to feed the family at the same time, during the Depression, is beyond me.

But he did.

The trouble with getting that many dogs together at one place is that they pass from one to the other any disease one may have, such as mange. Or they can all start taking fits at the same time, especially in the hot months of July or August.

But the thirty-six were there. Dad had many of them tied by chain to bushes above our house.

It was late July. It was hot.

On a Saturday afternoon Dad was gone.

But the dogs were there. And Walt and I were there.

One of the dogs started frothing at the mouth. It was not rabies. It was a kind of stomach trouble where the dog had a fit and it ran and barked wildly and foamed at the mouth. It seemed to have lost all the sense it ever had.

One dog doing that would not have been so bad. But when it does, that excites all the other dogs and soon the whole gang is into it.

That is exactly what happened.

The dogs which were loose and untied got into the act, barking and foaming at the mouth and running around crazily, in circles, without any logic at all.

And then the tied dogs broke loose. Pretty soon we had thirty six dogs with fits, foaming at the mouth, barking, running into each other and into the side of the house and under the house floor and into each other.

It was utterly crazy.

Mom and our sister Irene were in the house. So were Walt and I and our brother Carroll.

Walt and I decided to take over as we usually did when Dad was gone.

What we had in mind was to bring some order to the melee, to bring some common sense to the world outside the house and to get the flow of traffic going in one direction.

We went out to the wood yard and we each found a pole we could handle. We then entered the fray.

Mom and Sis were inside, screaming at us to get back inside. They thought all the dogs had rabies, were mad and were going to bite us and pass on the rabies.

Walt and I ignored that. We set to work. In a short while we had all the dogs running in the same direction. They were running around the house and were not running into each other or into the walls of the house or into any object.

Soon they slowed down and the noise got much quieter. Then they started pulling off from the crowd and lying down.

We took those with chains who had stopped and tied them up again.

In a very short time, we stopped the stampede.

But Mom and Sis still were not happy.

They thought we were more crazy than the dogs.

41

Hemlock Juice

When Dad got so many dogs together in the summer, they would pass along to each other the worst thing they could —mange.

Mange is a disease which will take the hair off a dog and, if untreated, will even take the skin off.

Dad would get lots of dogs together. Then, without knowing it, he would bring in one with the mange. Then the mange would spread among all of them.

I would know when that had happened. Dad would get me up early in the morning, and we would head for the woods with a double bitted axe and a spud.

The axe, of course, was for cutting down a tree, in this case, a hemlock tree.And the spud is an instrument by which you can peel bark from a tree.

Dad would select a hemlock tree, cut it with the double bitted axe and let it fall.

Then we would peel off the bark with the spud.

We would then carry the bark to our Early Harvest apple orchard where we kept our wash pot.

Our wash pot was a large, round, cast iron pot with a handle on top. It had three points on the bottom which could be placed on rocks to level it. A fire could then be built under it.

We put the hemlock bark in the pot and then finished filling the pot with water.

We started a fire under the pot and kept it going until we had boiled the water and the bark.

Then we removed the bark and we had remaining a pot full of hemlock juice.

Hemlock juice is potent. And it can cure mange on a dog. That is how it is used.

We tied up all the infected dogs and we took them one at a time and dipped them in the pot.

You have to be careful with that. A dog with mange dipped in hemlock juice will eat you up if he has a chance.

But we dipped them in and threw them out. When we did each dog would jump about ten feet.

It would yelp. And then, for some reason, it would head for the gap in the ridge where the road led over to Tuckasegee River. It would then jump about eight feet at a jump, up the hill, and disappear through the gap.

They would all be gone about three days. And then they would all come back, looking starved and dragging their tails, but all healed up and haired over. The mange had been cured.

42

"I Tole Ye I'd Meet Ye"

My Great Aunt Vice (pronounced Vicey) Hyde was my Great Grand father Ervin Hyde's sister. She married Quill Rose of Eagle Creek. Quill served in the Confederate Army under General Lee. He came back home to Eagle Creek and, among other things, made corn whiskey the rest of his life. His still was in the yard of his house, just as we might have a grill located today.

He didn't know that a law had been passed making it illegal to turn corn into whiskey.

He was eighty-one years old. One day while he was sitting on his front porch a United States Revenue Officer rode up. He got off his horse and came on the porch.

He asked Uncle Quill if he was making corn whiskey. Uncle Quill said that he was and that he had been making it all his life.

The Revenue Officer told him that that was illegal and he would have to arrest him and take him to court.

Uncle Quill told the Revenuer that he couldn't go that day but that he could meet him next morning at 7:00 o'clock at the depot over the hill at Proctor. With that the Revenuer drew his pistol and told Uncle Quill he would have to go right then.

The Revenuer was twenty-eight years old.

But Uncle Quill took the pistol away from the Revenuer, hit him over the head with it, knocking him out, and then carried the Revenuer to his horse, laid him over the saddle, tying his hands and feet underneath, then tied the bridle reins to the saddle horn and headed the horse back to Proctor.

The horse took his master home and he arrived there about 1:00 a.m. with a terrible head ache. Friends untied him and he wanted to go back that night and get Quill.

But friends warned him and talked him out of that.

Next morning at seven he started to ride by the depot at Proctor. There sat Quill.

Quill said: "I tole ye I'd meet ye here this mornin'."

Quill went to court and when questioned by the Judge about the kind of whiskey he made he said the very best.

He was placed on probation and continued to make corn whiskey the rest of his life.

43

Jay Hole

Logging in the mountains of Swain County took on some curious twists.

When logs needed to be moved down the mountain and when a cliff intervened, a special method had to be invented.

The ingenious mountaineer invented the method to handle it.

A mechanical device was invented to handle it. It was called a Jay Grab.

The Jay Grab was a device fastened to a chain which pulled logs and which would come loose when the animals pulling the chain which pulled the logs turned to the right.

That would allow the chain system connected to the animal pulling the log—usually a mule—to disconnect and allow the log to move forward when the animal turned right and disconnected itself from the log.

I had worked with Dad in logging and I knew the way the Jay Grab worked.

At the top of a cliff or steep slope in the path of the movement of logs, loggers would clear out an area to the right where the animal pulling the logs could turn right and disconnect the Jay Grab from the log load, allowing the logs to skid on down the mountain free from the chains connected with the pulling animals—steers or mules or what ever they were.

Mules or steers pulling logs under the circumstances described learned very quickly to turn right into the cleared path when the order "Jay Hole" was given. If they did not obey, they could be carried down the slope, and even over a cliff by the logs to which they were connected.

"Jay Hole" was, therefore, about the most important order in all logging in the hills. Dad had three mules. They were all trained to "Jay Hole." Somehow I got the notion that I could get all those mules to obey the order "Jay Hole" at one time.

All those mules were in a pasture below our house. Part of the pasture was a meadow along a branch with an apple tree in it.

I lined up the mules and then chased them and got them running down by the apple tree.

As they grew even to the apple tree, I would call "Jay Hole" and all three would turn right—right into that apple tree.

It was great fun until Dad caught me, gave me a whipping and explained to me that I was "injuring" his mules.

I hadn't thought of it that way.

But with the whipping I caught on.

I have been more careful with animals since then.

44

Just Checking On Folks

Gram Pa Medlin had only one eye. The other had been knocked out by a steer's horn hitting it.

He had only one good leg, too. The other was a peg leg, an actual wooden peg leg.

He had lost one leg when he fell from a lumber pile while working for W. M. Ritter Lumber Company at Proctor, North Carolina.

We all knew that his ability to carry on even ordinary tasks was limited.

It came a deep snow about the time I was thirteen years old. Dad was gone again to logging camp. Walt wasn't home.

I was the only one in our home who could help out.

Mom was worried about Gram Pa and Gram Ma Medlin. She directed me to walk over the hill to check on them.

I did so.

In my journey to do so, I walked through drifts of snow five feet high.

When I got there, I found that Gram Pa and Gram Ma Medlin were fine.

They had milked the cow and fed all the animals. There was plenty of fire wood in. They had water and plenty of food.

I returned home. I was completely exhausted.

Mom mentioned to me that perhaps Gram Pa and Gram Ma Hyde might need help. Of course, Aunt Ruth and Uncle Horace were still there to help them.

I pleaded off. And, as it turned out, I was right. That extra, dangerous two mile trip was not necessary.

But I still appreciate the concern that was shown by my Mom.

45

You Can't Hit a Bat

I wish someone had told me way back then the difference between a bat and a bird.

But they didn't.

Now I know the difference and it is considerable and important.

The bat is a mammal and it is not a bird.

The Cherokee Indians recognized the difference and recorded it in one of their beautiful myths.

But I did not know that as a boy, and as a boy I was an expert at rock throwing. I was the only boy in the county who was known for throwing a rock and killing a rattlesnake by hitting it between the eyes with a rock just as it placed its head over the root of a tree.

So it disturbed me that I could never hit a bat with a rock even though I could hit a snake, possums, squirrels and birds—but never a bat.

It was only when I learned in the Navy about radar that I fully appreciated why I could not hit a bat with a rock. It is just that the folks around me didn't know that bats had radar.

46

Aunt Annie, I Have Done Killed the Devil!

Even though for years I had watched bats flying, I had never seen one up close. I had no notion of what one looked like upon close inspection.

So it should not be hard to understand that when I finally did get to see one up close, I had no notion of what it was.

And I certainly did not know that it would fit exactly into my image of what the Devil looked like in every respect except size.

At the time, I was staying with Mom's sister, Aunt Annie Franklin, and her family. One of my duties was to cut wood for the fire place and the cook stove.

Late one fall afternoon I took a double bitted axe and walked from Aunt Annie's house out to a place called Jackson "Holler." There I set in to cut some dry wood for the cook stove.

I found a standing, dead white oak tree. It was not large, being only about five inches in diameter at the ground. The tip of the tree and some limbs near the top had fallen off to the ground.

I set in to chop it down. About the third time the axe hit the tree near the ground, a part of the top broke off and fell to the ground.

It made a loud thump and I saw some object bounce out of a hole in that part of the tree when it hit the ground. That object lay there motionless.

The sun was about to set in the west but it was shining brightly on that spot and on that object. It was so bright that the object seemed to be iridescent.

I thought I could see a skeleton inside that object and it looked like the skeleton of a man. But it was only a few inches in size. And it appeared to be lying on its back with its arms outstretched. It was not as big as a cat bird or a blue jay. But it was not a bird because it had no feathers.

Then I noticed that it seemed to have two horns and sharp teeth. Those horns were signs of the Devil. The sharp teeth confirmed that even more.

I looked again and it had two feet and those appeared to be split or cloven.

Those were sure signs of the Devil. I had heard that hundreds of times from local preachers in revival meetings.

That was enough for me.

It wasn't as big as I thought the Devil would be.

But it was the Devil.

I had no doubt.

And it was dead. I was sure of that. It had died when the broken tree hit the ground.

I yelled: "I have killed the Devil."

And I thought that I had saved the world.

I grabbed the object. I left the axe and the wood and I started running to the house.

Aunt Annie was in the yard.

I ran up, held out the object and shouted to her "Aunt Annie, I done killed the Devil."

She took one look and then yelled at me "That's a bat. Throw that thing down. If it bites you it will poison you deader than a door nail."

I threw it down.

And then I discovered that I had made another mistake.

It wasn't really dead. It began to move.

In a short while, it stood up and stretched out its arms.

Then it flew away.

But while it was stretching, I noticed a third factor.

Its feet were not cloven. It had toes and fingers.

That did it. According to all I had ever heard the Devil had cloven or split feet or hooves. He also had horns and sharp teeth but the cloven hoof was the real mark.

So it was not the Devil. And it was not dead. I had not killed the Devil. I had not saved the world.

I had learned a little more about bats but mostly I had learned something about not jumping to conclusions too quickly, especially if I were dealing with the Devil or thinking I had found a way to save the world all by myself, or declaring life or death for something I didn't know I had ever seen before, didn't know its name and really didn't know how to describe it.

It was a lesson well learned.

47

Getting Under the Tent Just to See the Camel's Nose

At my young age and in what really was a remote and isolated region it is no wonder that I had never even heard of a circus. Then one came to Bryson City, the county seat.

We heard about it and I decided to go see it on Saturday.

It was summer and the weather was nice. It was an easy walk to town.

And it wasn't hard to find where the circus had camped out. The crowds just led one there.

But I was in for a surprise.

The circus was located in a flat field. The front and the sides were fenced off. Tents were located in the back, blocking any entry that way. There was a gate in front and the crowd went through the gate.

But you had to pay a dime to get in. That was the surprise to me.

And I didn't have a dime. So I stepped back and I looked over the field.

I decided to go to the back where the tents were located to find out what else I could see. There was no fence back there. The circus people depended on the tents to block any entry back there.

But I found that the tent flaps were loose and one could crawl under them.

I gave it a try.

And I got inside the tent on my knees. Just as I did, a large nose with large eyes and large ears above came swinging around right into my face.

I had never seen a camel. But that was what it was. It was lying there under the tent.

And it confronted the intruder.

At my young age I had never heard of the poem called "The Camel's Nose" and I had never heard the expression that if you let a camel get its nose under a tent the camel would certainly come in.

Therefore, I didn't know that I was in a position flatly reverse to that .

But that didn't matter.

I got out of there. And I didn't get back into that circus at all.

I didn't see another camel for a long time. But when I did, I knew I had met one before, and up close at that.

48

Taking Off Warts

A man named Bart lived in our community. Part of the gossip that went around was that his wife was a witch and he was a warlock. It was said that if he got mad at anyone he would walk the road near where their cow was grazing and put a spell on the cow. At the next milking that cow gave bloody milk.

But it was also said that he could cure warts.

I got some warts on my hands and I wanted them off.

I saw Bart walking up the road one day and I stopped him. I told him that I had heard he could heal warts, that I had some and I wanted him to take them off.

He asked me to show them and I did.

He took my hands into his hands and told me to shut my eyes. He told me that if I kept my eyes shut while he rubbed the warts and didn't open my eyes until he told me to do so, the warts would go away in three days. For some reason I believed him.

He rubbed each wart, then dropped my hands and told me to open my eyes. I did.

He walked on his way.

In three days my warts were gone.

I thought a long time about the whole matter - about the gossip concerning cows giving bloody milk, about my warts going away and about his wife being a witch.

I had never seen anything strange about his wife. She was a very friendly person and she went to our church and took part in the singing. She went to Decoration Day at Watkins Graveyard and acted like everyone else there.

Then, too, I figured that nobody had any proof that Bart had anything to do with their cows giving bloody milk on occasion. He didn't touch their cows. And I heard people who didn't know Bart talk about their cows giving bloody milk on occasion. Finally, I came to the conclusion that his touching and rubbing the warts on my hands didn't cause them to go away. What caused that was his getting me to believe they would go away in three days.

Once I had made my mind up about that, my mind then sent the proper message to whatever part of my body could fight warts. And it worked.

I had no scientific proof then of the truth of that and I have none now.

But I still believe it.

49

The Words of Gram Pa Hyde

Gram Pa Hyde didn't pretend to have any formal education. And his use of the English language left a lot to be desired.

He occasionally used words that I never heard anyone else use. I had trouble in learning the meaning of some words he used and great difficulty in learning how he put some of them together.

Two such words were particularly bothersome to me. It took me years to find the real meaning and derivation of the two.

Finally I found at least part of the explanation in Horace Kephart's "Our Southern Highlanders" and the dictionary.

The first word was "fernent," as he pronounced it.

I was with Gram Pa Hyde in his tobacco patch behind his barn. I asked him where the cow was. He replied: "Fernent the barn."

I went to the other side of the barn and saw the cow in front of the barn and alongside it. By knowing that I came close to knowing the meaning of the word.

What I learned was that the word comes from Scotch. It is formed from two words: "fore" (mis-pronounced "fer" by many mountain people) which of course means "in front of" and "anent" meaning alongside.

The second word I had trouble with is a word Gram Pa Hyde used to describe a 17 year locust to me. I saw one and asked him what it was. He said it was a "ferro." Years later I found that word in Kephart with a question of whether or not it meant "Pharoah." Of course it does.

The locust was one of the plagues of Egypt.

50

Ride a Calf—Then Carry It

Dad took me and Walt with him over to Peach Tree one Saturday morning. He rode his bay mare and Walt and I walked behind him. There was good reason for that. Dad had to travel on to the head of Noland Creek to work out a trade on some cattle. In fact, he didn't get back home until dark. Walt and I got back in the middle of the afternoon.

But not without trouble.

Dad took us to a home on Peach Tree Creek and traded for a young bull calf. He told me and Walt to take it home.

We had a halter on it and a rope attached to the halter. We taught it to drive, that is, to go ahead of us, to stay in the road and to keep walking. We drove it down the creek to the Tuckaseigee River, up the river past Epps Spring and on up to the mouth of Lands Creek. We made good time.

Then after we had turned up Lands Creek to go by Gram Pa Hyde's house and then up the branch to our house, Walt said he thought he would ride the bull. The bull didn't resist. Perhaps it was too tired to resist. Walt rode a while and then got off and I rode a while. We rotated until we reached a point just below Gram Pa Hyde's house. Then we quit riding and drove the bull by the house of Gram Pa Hyde, up to the mouth of Emma Branch and started up that trail along that branch.

We reached the steepest part, that part of the old road taken away years ago by a slide.

Here the bull stopped. It wouldn't go forward. We tried every way we knew to get it to move. No success. Finally the bull calf lay down. It wouldn't get up.

We had a problem.

If we didn't get it home, we would have to tell Dad the truth - that each of us had ridden it. And we both knew that we should not have done so. It was too young to be ridden and we had worn it out. There was only one answer to the problem. It was a tough answer but it worked. We both took hold of the bull calf, lifted it up and carried it over the bad part of the trail. In fact we carried it all the way to the spring where Shep bayed the pheasant. From there on the road was level and clear. When we laid the bull calf down, it got to its feet and marched right on to our barn and we put it in a stall. We fed it and gave it water.

The calf never showed any adverse effect from being ridden. And we never told Dad about it.

Also, we never rode another bull calf that young again.

51

Caught By a Hawk—Make Him Bring You Back Home

It was while we were at the house of the owner of the calf we later rode that Walt and I heard the story of a real champion Banty rooster.

The man there was telling the story to Dad but we all listened.

He said that he had this one Banty rooster which he was so proud of. It was a bright colored, fine crowing king of the roost. The hens just loved it. And every other rooster around there held it in awe.

It could whip a rooster three times its size. And it could out crow a game rooster or even a Dominecker.

He said he had shelled some corn early that week and had thrown out some for the chickens near the barn. As he stood there he saw a shadow and looked up to see a large chicken hawk coming down toward the chickens. The hawk seemed to be diving at a great speed. It swooped and caught that champion Banty rooster and rose in the air. The owner could see the little Banty fighting but on the hawk flew and then went down out of sight on a ridge about one half mile away.

I saw the owner wipe tears from his eyes.

He said he stood in sadness and started to turn and go to the house.

Then he saw some movement on that far ridge. Something rose in the air and it was coming toward him. He watched. In a very short time the object came down to the ground, in front of him, only a few feet away. And suddenly there was that hawk setting that champion Banty Rooster down on the ground.

The hawk was in bad shape, missing feathers from its neck, its wings and its tail.

The Banty rooster walked around, shuffling his wings and then it stopped and crowed.

"I was so proud," the man said. "Not only did that little Banty Rooster whup the daylights out of that big old chicken hawk, why, he even made it bring him back home."

52

Picking Plums

A short time after we rode the bull calf, Walt and I were back on the water shed of Peach Tree. But we didn't follow the road. Uncle Lige Lowe, the Baptist preacher who preached at Rock Creek Baptist Church, owned a field on the side of a steep hill over-looking Peach Tree Creek and Tuckaseigee River. The field comprised about eight acres. Some years before that time some one had planted a big orchard of plum trees covering that field. Uncle Lige allowed us to pick plums free there.

When harvest time for plums came, Mom knew because we had one plum tree near our house.

Mom directed me and Walt to go to the orchard of Uncle Lige Lowe and to pick plums.

She gave each of us a meal sack and a gallon bucket.

Her instructions were to pick the plums and to place them in a bucket and, when the bucket was full, to pour them—very carefully—into the meal sack. She told us to get a load that was not too heavy to carry all the way home and to carry the sack—very carefully—back home. It was a tough trip. The shortest route was to walk down to Gram Pa Hyde's, then up a small branch, through his pasture, to his eight acre corn field, up by the field to a gap in the ridge and then down a short distance to the orchard.

We carried out the orders as given.

And we got the ripe plums home. Even so, many of them were squashed flat.

That didn't bother Mom. She took over and made use of all we had brought.

The end result was fine.

But neither Walt nor I ever volunteered to go back to that place for plums.

And we never again received orders to do so.

53

Catching Fleas

Walt and I had a much worse experience on Peach Tree. This happened in late July.

We had delivered a dog for Dad to a man who lived right at the head of Peach Tree. It was in the middle of a Saturday afternoon. As we came back down the creek, a thunderstorm swept over us. Thunder crashed all around us. Lightning was flashing all around us. And a torrent of rain was falling on us.

We knew the lightning was dangerous. And we didn't like getting soaked. A dwelling was close by. We ran onto the front porch. We were surprised to see a whole family sitting there in rocking chairs, all as calm as one could get.

In addition, their hound dogs were lying here and there on the floor.

The family welcomed us. We told them we appreciated that.

Then suddenly the storm slacked off. No more thunder and no more lightning and much less rain. I was delighted.

Just then I noticed something else. Fleas were hopping all over my bare arms, on my neck and on my face. I looked at Walt. The same was happening to him.

I looked at the several members of the family. There were no fleas on them.

Perhaps these were fleas who came out just to welcome strangers.

I told Walt we'd better be on our way. He agreed. We thanked our hosts and we left.

We were still getting wet as we walked on down the road but we were also getting rid of the fleas.

What a relief!

I have never yet figured out why we attracted fleas but our hosts didn't.

54

Sam and the Twist

Life was tough in those Depression years. There didn't seem to be much money, or if there was, those who had it were not talking about it and certainly were not spreading it around.

There was no lack of work to be done. There was all I could do and then some. It was just that you couldn't get money for work. That was the rub.

There were a few enterprises one could enter for profit. In the summer blackberry picking was lucrative. At ten cents a gallon I could make a dollar in a long day. But most of the time I was not free to operate. Mom canned most of the berries. It was only on occasion that I was allowed to carry berries to town for sale. And, even then, the take was not all mine. Basic groceries were needed and these came from the berry money and the butter and egg money.

When I was seven and Walt was nine, we managed to get enough money to start two enterprises. We tried tobacco farming on a small scale. It wasn't burley; it was broadleaf tobacco, which you could make into twists for chewing. It brought a dime a twist. We earned every penny of it, what with the hoeing and the worming and the suckering and the cutting and the twisting and the selling.

After we cut the tobacco and hanged it to cure, we advertised. It was just general word of mouth, but it worked. They came from all around and bought. Most bought one twist at a time. Walt and I decided to encourage bulk buying and offered three twists for a quarter. Sometimes we could sell six to one customer that way.

I remember when we had only twelve twists left. We had them on a string in the barn loft corner, with a loop in each end of the string and these attached over a nail on each side. The customer would pay and then take a twist from either end of the string.

When Walt and I were first learning how to make a twist, we goofed on one and made it about three times as big as the rest. We laid it aside until we were down to about the last dozen and then put it in the middle of the string with the other, smaller twists on each side.

Shortly after that, Sam came in.

Sam was a droll sort of fellow. He had a big frame and it always moved slow in every part. He didn't work much, and when he did, he never overdid it. He walked slow, he sat down slow, he got up slow. Work was his private enemy number one; speed ran a close second. After observing him a few times, I knew that if he ever did move fast, he would break every bone in his body.

His speech was no traitor to all his other outward appearances. His words came seldom, in small lots, and then reluctantly, lazily, limpid and drawn out.

I had not seen his approach, but I heard his slow, heavy tread on the steps leading to the loft. "Howdy," he said.

"Howdy, Sam."

"Is 'zat 'baccer much 'uh punkin?" he asked, one eye on me and the other divided between Walt and the string in the corner.

That one threw me. To put tobacco and pumpkins in the same category wasn't my idea of good taste. Nevertheless, it was good tobacco. So I answered him.

"It shore is," I said.

"How much a twist?" he asked, and turned his head sideways either to hear better or to get a better look at the shadowed corner.

"Dime a twist," Walt said.

Sam fumbled in his pocket and finally brought out a dime, black with age and with a recent close association with plug tobacco.

"Here," he said, handing Walt the dime with his left hand while employing his right hand to bring out a long, bone handled, hawk billed knife.

At first his purpose wasn't clear to me. Most buyers would first get their twist and then bring out their Barlow or other of several assorted knives to cut off a good chew from the tip of the twist. But here was Sam with his knife out before he even got the twist.

He advanced slowly to the corner. Then with unusual speed for him he raised the knife. The left hand grasped the over-sized twist in the middle. With one deft flick the hawkbill bit through the round end of the twist freeing it to slip off the string. He then shoved it in his shirt pocket, big end down, the little end of the twist coming up to about shoulder level.

Sam had 30 cents worth of "baccer" for only a dime.

"Youns come," he said, as he sauntered over the loft and down the steps. We didn't answer. His hat disappeared from sight.

Walt and I looked at each other.

"Darn," Walt said.

It was enough said.

Ever since then I've been wary of big, slow moving, slow talking people. When I deal with one of them, I remember that big twist and just figure that they never let their talking get ahead of their thinking. I watch them close. It pays.

55

A Hoe Hoeing Corn By Itself

Fide Hyde was my Dad's uncle, the brother of my Gram Pa Hyde. We all called him Uncle Fide. He was not the steady worker that Gram Pa Hyde was and he did not attend church regularly as Gram Pa Hyde did.

But he was truly a world of fun. He didn't take much seriously.

According to Gram Pa Hyde, when he and Fide and their brother, Mike Hyde, were young men, they traveled from one home to another, taking part in music and square dances. Gram Pa Hyde picked the banjo, Mike Hyde played the fiddle and Fide Hyde called the square dances.

Fide loved corn whiskey. Gram Pa Hyde may have done the same when he was young but he never touched any during my life.

Uncle Fide played jokes on people around him all the time.

Somehow I became one of his favorites.

Gram Pa Hyde had an eight acre corn field in Coon Cove, above his house, on the west side of the hollow, on a steep hill side. It was dark, rich soil and it grew tall stalks and big healthy ears of corn. The ground was very rocky.

We had to hoe the corn—that is cut out the weeds with a hoe— at least three times a season and usually four times.

Gram Pa Hyde had to have a lot of help in tending that field. When it came time to hoe, Dad, Walt, I and my brother Carroll helped. Mom came and helped Gram Ma Hyde cook dinner for all the helpers. She brought the other children.

Uncle Fide Hyde came and brought his son Joe, who usually plowed between the corn rows with a mule pulling the plow. Uncle Fide's wife, Aunt Bessie and his three daughters also came and helped with the cooking.

Uncle Fide and Gram Pa Hyde joined in hoeing the corn.

Each of us had a hoe. When noon came, we each dug the hoe into the ground at the end of the field, covering the blade with dirt and leaving the handle sticking up.

I was told that this was necessary to keep the hot sun from "drawing the mettle" out of the hoe, that is, heating up the blade and making it softer so that it would dull more easily.

Uncle Fide added to the education I was receiving.

He told me that if I held my mouth just right when I dug my hoe in to leave it, the hoe would hoe corn by itself while I was gone.

He said he always did that.

I didn't know it for a long while but I learned that, after he told me that, he would slip off ahead of us after we ate dinner, hurry back to the corn field and hoe some corn before the rest of us got back.

He would point out to me when I got back that there was more corn hoed then than there was when we left. He said his hoe did it.

I kept trying to hold my mouth right, twisting it this way and that.

I hope that that didn't have anything to do with my later becoming a lawyer or taking part in politics.

But I never could get my mouth right.

Then one day I slipped off early after dinner and I heard someone coming and I hid.

It was Uncle Fide. He grabbed his hoe where he had left it (I had already seen that) and he quickly hoed several hills of corn. Just as we could hear the others returning, he ran and dug his hoe in the ground again, the handle sticking up.

As the rest crowded in, I slipped into the crowd and when Uncle Fide saw me, he pointed at his hoe and the extra hills he had hoed and told me his hoe did that while he was gone.

I then told him I saw him hoe that corn. I told him I had come on ahead and had hidden and watched him when he came.

He saw I had him. But that didn't bother him. I think that was what he had been waiting for. He laughed and laughed and laughed. He laughed so hard that he lay down and rolled.

I just stood there, moving my mouth around in all kinds of shapes.
He saw that.
He laughed even more.
It was impossible to keep him from having fun.

56

Hoop Snakes

Before I was able to prove that it was only a myth that holding your mouth right while you dug a hoe in the ground would get your corn hoed free, Uncle Fide had already sold me on another myth.

This one was worse. It was scary.

Our mountains were the home of the large chestnut trees. Some would grow a hundred feet tall and have a diameter at the trunk over eight feet.

We harvested the chestnuts. And our hogs ran in the woods and grew fat on the chestnuts.

But disaster struck. The chestnuts started dying.

I didn't know the cause. No one talked about it.

It was a long while before I learned that a blight had been brought in from overseas and that it would kill almost all our chestnut trees.

Other trees also died. Lightning struck some trees, killing them. Seventeen year locusts would strip some trees. Bugs invaded other trees.

Uncle Fide gave me a different story. That was typical of him. He had a lot of fun carrying on with me about it for a long time.

What he told me was that there were large hoop snakes (that is what he called them) in the mountains.

These snakes all had a horn on their backs about three or four inches from the ends of their tails. Those horns would grow to be as much as three inches in height.

The hoop snake would crawl up a mountain or ridge to the very top. There it would coil up (Uncle Fide said it would "quile up") in a round hoop, like a wheel, taking the end of its tail into its mouth up to the horn. Then it would turn to roll down the mountain, like a wheel, with the horn sticking out ready to hit something.

And whatever that horn hit was killed instantly. It didn't matter what it was: a bear, a coon, a possum, a hog, a tree, a little boy or anything else.

When we would walk along a ridge or up a creek road, Uncle Fide would point out to me dead trees and say the hoop snake had done that.

We had two highly poisonous snakes in the mountains, the rattle snake and the copperhead. I had seen several of each kind. And I was very careful not to allow one to bite me. Such a bite would be deadly.

But what could I do to prevent a hoop snake from hitting me?

I walked around for months watching out for hoop snakes, looking all around and staying alert so that if I had to, I could run or dodge or get out of the way somehow.

Then I spoke to one of my teachers and told him that the hoop snakes were killing a lot of our trees. He had never heard of the hoop snake but he said that a disease was killing our chestnut trees, not snakes.

That was the fall after I had solved the mystery of the hoe.

The next time I saw Uncle Fide, I told him about the disease killing the chestnut trees. He had never heard of such a disease he said, but he got a big laugh out of it.

57

Sycomore or Sycamore

Shortly after I first learned to read, I read the Book of Amos in the King James version of the Bible. I found that Amos said that he was not a prophet nor the son of a prophet but a herdsman and a gatherer of "sycomore" fruit.

We had trees in the Smoky Mountains growing along streams of water which the old folks told me were sycamore trees. At least that is what I thought.

And those trees were peculiar. The bark seemed always to be coming off and the trees were white in spots. And those trees grew round pods, brown in color, on a stem a little larger than the glass marble we played the game of marbles with. But that was a seed pod. It was not a fruit, at least as I understood what fruit was—a thing you could eat fresh from the trees.

So, after reading that part of Amos, I walked for miles along the Tuckaseigee River, Lands Creek, Forney Creek, Noland Creek and a large number of branches, trying to find sycamore fruit.

I could find none.

Then I looked at a dictionary and I found that, in fact, the "sycomore" tree had a fig like fruit but there was no mention of the American tree "sycamore" having any such fruit.

That taught me a lesson. Since then I've tried not to assume too much. I haven't always been successful but I still try.

58

Coke is Not For Preachers

Walt and I had worked hard. We had been at it all week long and had carried out our usual duties: feeding the stock, milking the cow, feeding the dogs, bringing in water from the spring, cutting stove wood, feeding the chickens and helping with the washing.

We had delivered the Grit Magazine to our customers on Friday. Then we had picked blackberries on Saturday and carried gallons to town and sold them.

We had collected a little cash.

To celebrate we went to Mr. Sneed's Grocery Store in town and we each paid a nickel for a Coca Cola.

Present in the store was a neighbor we knew. He had lately become a preacher although, to my own knowledge, he couldn't read very well at all.

He saw us buy the Coca Colas. He came over to us.

"It is a sin," he said "to drink Coca Cola." Quite frankly I didn't know what he meant and, just as frankly, I didn't care.

I continued to drink my coke. So did Walt. The preacher walked away.

Then Walt explained it to me.

"He doesn't have a nickel," he said. "He can't buy a Coca Cola for himself so he tells us that it is a sin to drink one."

I got the point.

And ever since then I have been a bit slow in accepting what some preachers say about some things.

59

Shooting a Swiss

I knew there were many different kinds of guns. Dad traded guns with neighbors. He got an automatic Colt .45 pistol from a man who had served in the Army in Panama. He possessed scores of shot guns over the years, swapping them in and out. Rifles were the same way.

But, so far as I recall, he owned only one Swiss rifle. And he traded it to a friend the very day he brought it home.

Maybe I had something to do with that trade taking place so quickly. Dad brought the gun in from town. Shortly after Dad got home, a friend came by and Dad showed him the rifle. I was looking, too. I asked Dad to let me shoot the rifle. His friend urged him to oblige. It was a bolt action gun. And it was big and heavy. The stock was too long to fit against my shoulder and give me room to pull the trigger. So I placed the stock under my right shoulder and squinted along the barrell. Both Dad and his friend were helping. They stood close and helped me point the barrel toward a large yellow pine tree up the hill.

I aimed. I pulled the trigger. The gun fired. The bullet tore a large slab off the yellow pine tree.

But that wasn't the big thing.

I knew a shotgun would kick when you fired it and the bigger the gun the harder it kicked.

But I didn't know any rifle would kick.

I learned.

That rifle kicked so hard that the bolt came back, hit me in the shoulder and knocked me to the ground.

I wasn't really hurt.

But Dad's friend thought it was hilarious. He laughed and helped me up and patted me on the back.

He bought the gun from Dad right then and paid him cash for it. He had eyewitness proof that it was a powerful weapon.

And that it surely was—on both ends.

60

Bury a Dead Mule Twice

Our Aunt and Uncle who lived in the house below us in Emma Field moved over to Rainbow Springs in Macon County. The lumber company which was located first at Proctor for twenty years pulled out and went to Rainbow Springs.

Our Uncle had worked for that company in their sawmill at Proctor and he picked up the same job when the company moved.

A cousin of Mom's moved into the lower house. She and her first husband had lived in Georgia for many years, They were divorced and she took their three children.

After a while she met a gentleman who had lived in Chicago about all his life. But, somehow, he traveled to Georgia and met her there. They were married and they had twin sons.

With their five children they moved into that lower house.

The husband was trying to support the family by running the place as a farm and by selling pulp wood, acid wood, cross ties, tan bark and some of the crops they could grow.

He had a tough time of it.

Dad and Walt and I helped him out when we could. Mom and the younger children helped when they could.

But he simply did not know the ways of running such a mountain farm.

One particular incident sticks in my memory.

Dad had helped him trade for a mule and to get it at a low price. There was a good barn on the place and a good pasture. He worked the mule every way he could.

The mule was far from young. And it may be that he did not feed it properly. That I don't know.

But the mule came down with something. And, in a couple of days, it died.

Its owner came to our house and asked to borrow our mule to pull the dead mule off where he could bury it.

Dad was not at home. But Walt and I geared up Dad's mule and turned it over to him.

We didn't know that he planned to bury the dead mule in the lower part of our pasture. We didn't go with him and we didn't know until he brought Dad's mule back what he had done.

He mentioned where he had buried the mule. He said he hit solid rock and had a hard time getting the job done.

Walt and I went and looked.

What he had said was not quite accurate. He didn't really get the job done at all.

What we found was a pile of brush placed on top of a shallow grave where the mule lay on his back, partly covered by dirt but with his four stiff legs sticking up through the dirt and the brush.

Young as we were we knew that a disaster was pending.

Dad was due home that night so we decided to wait and tell him and work out what to do.

It was dark when Dad got home. It was mid summer. After we explained the matter to Dad he said we could wait until morning but that we would have to do something next day.

He was right because we did something next day but even then the green flies were all around us as we worked. Had we let a few days go by, every person in that hollow could have been in mortal danger. That is what Dad told us.

We removed the brush. We dug out enough dirt so that we could get a rope around the mule's neck. We then hitched it to the gear on Dad's mule and he pulled out the dead mule.

We drove Dad's mule across the meadow, out of our pasture and up a hollow to our corn field where I had found the Indian spear head under a large flint rock.

There we unhitched the dead mule and Dad drove his mule to our barn, took off the gear and then came back. He showed me and Walt where to dig a grave immediately below where the dead mule lay. He went on to other work around the place.

Walt and I started digging. It took us all the rest of the day. Just before supper time, Dad came back and said the hole was fine. We rolled the dead mule into the hole and then started covering it up with the dirt.

That didn't take nearly as long as the digging had taken but it was late when we finished.

Walt and I were exhausted. But a real health hazard had been removed.

Walt expressed our feelings very well when he told Dad that he hoped our neighbor never got another mule—dead or alive.

61

Dig a Hole, Dig a Hole

I learned a sad song while I was very young. It was called "Darlin' Cora" and its refrain was: "Dig a hole, Dig a hole in the meadow. Dig a hole in the cold, cold ground. Dig a hole, Dig a hole in the meadow. Goin' to lay Darlin' Cora down."

I thought of that song while we were giving the dead mule his second burial. And I thought of it even more when Gram Pa Medlin learned that Walt and I had dug the second grave and had done a good job.

He told Mom to send us over to his house. He and Gram Ma Medlin were living in a house close to where I was born. There was no spring near by. The closest spring was over a low ridge near another house. It was the head of Mountain Branch.

To get water for themselves, their chickens, their cat, their cow and their hog Gram Pa Medlin or Gram Ma Medlin had to walk over the ridge and carry water back in buckets.

It was a long, hard trip.

They had done the job for a long time but it was hard on them. And, I guess it seemed even harder as they grew older.

I knew that long trip for water was a great burden to him.

Walt and I went to see him as requested. He told us he had heard we were good diggers and he needed a well dug. He said he could pay us a little to do it. He showed us where he wanted it. It was at a spot very near his house.

Walt and I told him we were willing to try but we asked him to supervise us as we did. We also told him we wanted to talk to Dad about it to get any advice he could give us and also to work out a schedule about the work we were expected to do at home.

We talked to Dad. He advised us what tools to use and how to haul the dirt out as we dug the well deeper each day.

We started the job. We followed Dad's advice and we also followed the suggestions of Gram Pa Medlin. He was with us every day.

It took us three weeks at six days a week, from early until late. We got it done.

Our work included helping to build a well house over the well, which included a floor, a roof over that floor and a winch with a rope and a bucket and a handle to turn to draw the water bucket up when filled with water. Gram Pa Medlin did most of the carpentry work. Our job was mostly digging and hauling away the dirt.

It was a fine well. It was still working well the last I knew of it.

And our grandparents were really happy. We saved them both time and energy.

Gram Pa Medlin paid me and Walt. It wasn't much but we were happy.

That's the way to make things work.

62

Plumb Down I Fell

Somewhere along the line in my school years I learned that John Milton in "Paradise Lost" mentioned that "plumb down" the devil fell for nine days.

I never fell that long to my knowledge but I did fall "plumb down" one time.

It was the day after election day when Franklin D. Roosevelt was first elected president.

I didn't know anything about politics. But I had listened to the older people talk. And they were often at odds with each other. Some wanted the president who was in office to win again. Others wanted him out and wanted a new one.

As I listened, I began to take sides with the underdog. If the people I knew and heard talk about it had had the power to select, the incumbent would stay in.

That is why I wanted Roosevelt to win.

We didn't have a radio at our house so we didn't keep up well with the news. But there was a radio in the home of some of my cousins.

Walt and I were walking toward town to school. We were early and I climbed a persimmon tree.

Our cousins—also going to school—caught up with us. Their parents favored the incumbent president.

They had heard the news and they told Walt immediately that Roosevelt had been elected.

I heard it and I was happy my hero had won.

I started to clap. That was stupid. My hold on the tree was gone and plumb down I fell.

But it wasn't far and I wasn't hurt.

But I was embarrassed.

And I guess that is why I have remembered ever since then where I was when I learned that Roosevelt was elected.

63

I Was There

My uncle, father of the cousin who reported the election of Roosevelt to me and Walt, drove a "For Hire" pick up truck to make a living.

Many years after that day, President Roosevelt was scheduled to come to Newfound Gap, in the heart of the Smoky Mountains, on the line separating North Carolina and Tennessee, to dedicate the Great Smoky Mountains National Park.

My uncle offered to let me and his son ride with him to witness the affair.

We went. It was wonderful.

I thought that there were at least ten thousand people present, covering the whole gap and both sides of the mountain. For the first time in my life, I saw a multitude.

To me it was truly a momentous occasion. To see and hear the President of the United States there in my native mountains was almost unbelievable. But most of all, it was so good finally to see the man whose announcement of victory caused me to fall plumb down.

64

My First Suit

It was the Spring after that when I bought my first suit.

The occasion for that great event was my graduation from grammar grade, the end of the seventh grade. And I was to be crowned King in a ceremony honoring me as the boy with the highest grades along with a girl crowned Queen, honoring her as the girl with the highest grades.

I never had worn a suit. But Dad and Mom said it was necessary for the occasion.

There were three dry good stores in Bryson City. Solomon Maloof owned one. That is where I went to get my new suit.

Mom helped me pick it out. Dad was with us. It was pure wool, dark in color, with a double breasted coat.

With it I had to have a belt, a white shirt, a tie and a pair of dress shoes.

All that cost seven dollars and a half. I only had a dollar and a half. But Mr. Maloof gave me credit for the rest. It took me half the summer selling blackberries and stove wood and Grit magazines but I paid it off six weeks after I finished the seventh grade and was crowned King.

It was worth it.

65

The Bull and the One Who Would Stand

Dad traded around and got a steer that was big enough to work. Dad had sold his last mule and we had no animal to pull a sled, to snake a log of wood to the wood yard or to plow when we needed to plow.

Dad was off at work at a logging camp. There was no one home to teach that steer how to plow or pull a sled or snake a log, except Walt and me.

Dad had traded away all the working gear we could use on a mule or horse or steer except a McClellan saddle. And we had learned our lesson about that.

We didn't need to do any riding. What we needed was a trained, working steer.

All the gear left on the place was an ox yoke with the trace chains and single tree to go with it.

But an ox yoke is for two oxen or steers. It fits a team.

We didn't have a team. In truth, we were in a dilemma.

Walt suggested that maybe we could hitch him in on one side of the yoke with the steer and let him simply hold up that side of the yoke while the steer pulled the whole load.

We got the steer out of the barn, tied him, and hitched him into the yoke. Then I hitched Walt into the yoke on the other side. They were not yet hitched to a load.

I untied the steer. I hadn't more than done so when the steer took off. You would have thought he was trying to win the Kentucky Derby.

He ran through a field, then through a field of blackberry briars, then through some brush and bushes. Walt was trying to hang on and to protect himself the best he could.

I was running behind, crying, my heart breaking for the pain my brother was having.

Finally the bull reached the top of a ridge and he stopped, gasping for breath. I ran up and started to take Walt out of the yoke when Walt managed to blurt out, "Hey, Hub, take that bull out. I'll stand."

66

My *Gone Gun*

Before I joined the Navy in World War II and went off to fight in the Pacific, I only owned one gun. And that ownership probably set a record for the shortest ownership in history.

I worked hard for it. And I truly adored it as my first real possession of something that should only belong to a grown man.

Dad had a relative who owned and operated a corn mill in Bryson City. It was the first corn mill I ever saw which operated on electricity. It didn't have the mill dam and the wheel turned with the water from the dam.

And it operated much more efficiently and probably ground more corn in one day than one of those water powered mills could grind in a month.

The owner had no help and he told me he needed some help. He talked to Dad and Dad told him I could help him on a limited basis.

And so I started. I could work only a short time each day. But I kept it up.

I didn't have any agreement about pay. But in about six weeks the owner paid me for my labor. I had gotten him over the hump and he didn't need my help for a while.

My pay check was unusual.

He handed me a rifle—heavy, bolt action, 32-20, with an octagon shaped barrel. I had never seen anything like it.

I took it home with great pride.

Dad looked it over and then laid it in a gun rack in our hall. That was about dark the day I got it.

I left the next morning for school and I never saw that rifle again. Dad traded it away that day.

When I got home it was gone.

I knew that Dad had been trying to get a Walker Fox Hound from a friend for weeks. He just wasn't getting anywhere.

Dad had a reputation of being the best trader in that whole country. But his friend was holding out.

Finally Dad found what he needed: a heavy 32:20 bolt action rifle with an octagon shaped barrel.

He got his dog. And my gun was gone.

And what he got was not a pure-bred Walker. It was a part Walker. It was a female. She was small. And her voice was not great.

I thought of all of that.

I wondered why Dad wanted her.

But I found out pretty soon.

We went fox hunting soon after that. We had a lot of friends with us. Dad's brother, Horace, went. His uncle Fide went. Also present were Carl Fox, Gainey Burns and Taylor Sherrill.

Taylor Sherrill worked for the railroad. He had what was referred to as a public job. He lived close to us. He and his wife had several children, all girls. They were all still too young for school.

We went up on Basil Mountain, overlooking Peach Tree and the Tuckaseigee River. All that country is now in the National Park.

We built a camp fire and we waited. Soon the dogs struck up a fox.

Each dog owner knew his dog by its bark.

And each took pride when their dog barked, particularly when that dog was leading the pack.

Dad's new dog wasn't heard at first.

And then, suddenly, she was heard.

She was at the head of the pack.

And her bark was distinctive. You couldn't miss it.

It was evident that she was leading the pack. She kept it up. For three hours she led all those dogs on the trail of the fox.

Everyone was impressed.

How could a dog that young and that small—particularly a female —take over like that.

Trading talk started. All the men wanted Dad's dog—Taylor Sherrill in particular.

As the talk went on, Taylor Sherrill topped all the offers that had been made.

He offered Dad his only cow and his only hog for that one dog.

I had never heard anything like it. A cow and a hog were worth at least a dozen dogs.

But that was the offer. And Dad took it.

We left the hunt while the dogs were still out in the woods. Taylor Sherrill just had to trust to luck that little Walker would return.

We walked to Taylor Sherrill's house. We got there a little after daylight.

And I will never forget that scene.

That milk cow was the only cow that family had. She provided them with milk and cream and buttermilk and butter. Now she was going away.

And that hog was the only hog they had. One hog usually provided a family all kinds of pork products in the fall and winter when they needed it. Now that was going away.

It was an easy matter to take the cow away. She had a halter on her and I simply attached a rope to that and led her away.

Dad had to put a rope around the hog's front legs and teach it to walk ahead and he did that.

We left with our property.

But I will never forget the scene as I saw it. The little Sherrill children were all standing on the porch, leaning against the rails, as we took away their only source of milk and meat for winter. I thought about it very seriously but I didn't say a word.

I just gave up in my own mind any claim to my first rifle or to the dog Dad got in the trade or to the cow or the hog we were taking home.

I don't know how else I could have handled it. At least, that's the way I did it.

67

Have They Got You In Here, Too?

Dad's first cousin loved corn liquor. So did Dad. But that was not unusual. So did his cousin's dad, Uncle Fide.

And in their many years of handling that I learned many lessons. None of them were thieves; none of them were outlaws; none of them were liars. All of them were honest and most of them were hard working. All of them supported their families.

But funny things happened with them.

I remember the night that Dad's cousin came by. It was a winter night. He had been drinking—perhaps a little too much.

He sat by the fire place. Dad offered him a bed where he could sleep. But he said he would just sit by the fire.

He did sit by the fire. Time passed on. It got to about three o'clock in the morning and the fire had died down.

He was sleeping in his chair.

The moon was up and shining through the window and curtain near him. The window frame probably looked like prison bars with the moon shining through.

Then he woke up and made some comment. Dad was in bed but he heard him and he said: "What's going on?"

His cousin, seeing the window and the moon shining through and perhaps thinking he was in jail responded: "Hell, Ervin, have they got you in here too?"

68

Praying for Frank

Dad's cousin Frank often drank too much. And he never attended church to my knowledge. Yet he is the man who said, in my presence, that: "Ligion (Religion) on Lands Creek is a scace (scarce) article."

Mom was a devout Baptist. And she believed in prayer.

Frank came by our house with his young second wife. It was early evening. He told Mom he was worried about his soul and he needed prayer. And then he walked on toward his house.

He could drink a whole lot and still appear sober. He didn't appear drunk at that time. Dad came home and Mom told Dad about it.

Apparently Mom worried about it for just at dark she asked me to light an oil lantern and to carry it as I went with her to Frank's house.

We arrived and Mom knocked at the door. Frank's wife came to the door. Mom asked if Frank was there.

His wife said he was but he was asleep. Mom said she was worried about him and came to pray with him.

His wife responded that he had been drunk for three weeks and that he was not at all serious when he spoke to Mom earlier that day.

We turned and went home.

No one ever mentioned the incident again. I understood why.

69

Kick in the Dark

Even though I had promised myself years before that I would not kick blindly in the dark when I thought a cat was on my bed, I ran into another kicking incident at night.

I was spending some time at my Aunt Annie's home and traveling over to our house at night. Walt was gone by then and Dad was in a logging camp. Mom needed someone there at night.

I left Aunt Annie's house after dark one night. I had worked hard getting the cows milked and the stock fed, so I was running late.

It was a dark, dark night. And I was following a trail through the pasture then over the hill.

I was following that trail through a wooded part of the pasture. I knew the trail well enough to follow it, although I could not see it.

Then suddenly my foot hit an object in the trail. I heard a grunt. I reached down my hand and felt long hair on a warm body.

My first thought was that I had stumbled upon a black bear. And my first instinct was to persuade it to move out.

I hauled back my right foot and I kicked the unknown object. Then immediately I realized what I had kicked.

It was a cow lying in the trail.

But my instinct paid off and the kick worked. The cow got up and moved out of the way.

I went on.

But after that I started carrying a light at night. That was a wise move.

70

What a Blessing!

Gram Pa Medlin was a great blessing to me.

And he became such quite naturally.

Gram Pa Medlin was not a preacher. He was not a graduate of any college. Much like Amos, he didn't pretend to be a prophet or the son of a prophet.

But he was a blessing.

He was kind and considerate. He was understanding and compassionate. He knew human nature. And he knew what little boys needed.

He was a good reader. He taught me how to do that. He read me Aesop's fables. He brought his "Blue Back Speller" to my attention and I learned to read it.

While Granny Gouge taught me ghost stories and old songs, my Dad taught me about trees, and farm animals, Gram Ma Hyde taught me about herbs and medicines and Gram Ma Garrett taught me about Indian myths and Indian lore, Gram Pa Medlin taught me about ancient fables, about morals, about personal responsibility and about the facts of life.

It was from that "Blue Back Speller" that I learned so many truths: the world turning; surveying the starry heavens; wise men employ their time doing good to all around them; a good son will help his father; a good boy will learn to read and spell; avoid strong drink and gambling. It was from Aesop's Fables that I learned about the "Dog In The Manger" and scores of other stories about morals.

He showed me the evening star and the Big Dipper and the Little Dipper and dozens of other stellar wonders.

He told me how we got the Milky Way. And he is the only person I ever knew who knew the poem which told that story. He quoted it to me and I memorized it.

"The Man In The Moon
As he sails the sky
Is a Very Remarkable Skipper.
But he made a mistake
When he tried to take
A drink of milk with the Dipper.
He dipped it in with a careful hand
And he slowly and carefully filled it.
But the Big Bear growled
And the Little Bear howled
And scared him so that he spilled it."

I don't need any other explanation of the Milky Way.

71

Called to Bray

Starting at an early age, and going on and on, I heard preacher after preacher explaining how he had been "called to preach." I listened and I wondered.

And then one day I listened to a story which I truly believed.

It wasn't a sermon. It was a simple statement of facts by a Baptist preacher I had grown to respect and believe.

He was Mr. Hall. He had been preaching for fifty years.

And I don't know why he took up with me as he did. But he did. And he would come walking by our house and take me to the Revival at his church and walk back home with me.

He would tell me stories as the two of us walked to church. And he would tell me more stories as he walked me back home.

One day he said that he had a very important story to tell me but he didn't want me to repeat it while he lived. I promised.

And I kept my promise.

He said that before he started preaching he thought that he got a call from God to preach. And he started preaching and he had been at it fifty years.

But then—just recently—he thought back about that day.

It was a Sunday morning and he was walking to church. To take a shorter route he cut through a neighbor's pasture. And, as he walked along, he heard a sound and that was his call to preach.

But after thinking back over it recently it suddenly dawned on him that all he really heard was a mule braying.

But he had been at it so long he just kept it up.

After that I believed everything he told me.

72

Catching the Rainbow

We were living on Lands Creek on the old Jimmy Jenkins place. The town of Bryson City had acquired all the land on the watershed at the head of Lands Creek. They had built a dam and a reservoir for water so that the town could furnish inside water to the residences of its citizens.

I thought it was ironic. Not a single home on Lands Creek had inside water in the house. And, as far as I knew, not a single home in all of Swain County outside the county seat of Bryson City had inside water.

The water line from the dam ran down the creek and through our farm. I had seen the work crew place the pipe line in the ground.

I was just a boy. But I had noticed that the pipe line was not buried very deeply in the ground. The line ran along the creek and the road and through our garden and potato patch.

I was certainly no engineer. But I was acquainted with smoke houses where we kept our smoked and salted pork ham. Those houses were all above ground. There was no need to bring such smoke houses into the hillside because the pork stored there was preserved by smoking and salt and not by being buried in such a way as to keep from freezing.

On the other hand, our Irish potatoes were buried in a manner to keep them from freezing.

And—in a case more in point—our can houses contained hundreds of glass cans of black berries and many other berries and vegetables which had to be in a temperature above freezing. For that reason, we dug out sites for can houses back into a hill side and when we had completed the building of a can house, it was located back far enough into the ground that the temperature inside the can house would not fall below freezing. It was much like a natural cave where the temperature usually stays above fifty degrees.

Perhaps the people doing the work on the Bryson City water line were not well acquainted with such facts. They didn't bury the lines deep enough and so that winter when freezing came, the lines burst. In our potato patch, along the road and creek, parts of the burst line broke out on top of the soil.

There was a bill to pay in Bryson City.

But when Spring came the lines were opened up and new lines were buried much deeper.

But when the dam was first built and the reservoir was just filling up, the creek almost disappeared. There were branches running into Lands Creek below the dam so that a little water kept coming on down the creek. But for a while there was little creek there.

As a consequence, the fish headed for deeper holes and hid under rocks where they could.

I figured out immediately what was happening. And so I started at our lower line working my way up the creek, checking for fish in deep holes around rocks. And right away I found what I expected.

I found a Rainbow Trout—the biggest I had ever seen—about eighteen inches long. It was in a deep hole, under a rock. I grabbed it. And I held on. I got out of the creek and up the bank and on the way to the house.

I held on for dear life.

And I made it.

Dad and Mom were amazed.

We had a great supper.

After all, I had caught the Rainbow.

73

Snake, Don't Sneak Down My Back

The reservoir for the town finally filled up and we went back to normal.

On a Saturday morning, I took a fishing trip up the creek.

I was above the one room school house and Spruce Grove Baptist Church. I had been following the creek, hopping from rock to rock.

Above the school house where Silver Mine Branch ran into the creek, Bill Seay had a corn mill. I was a little way below his mill. Over head grape vines ran across the creek in the trees. I had found a good deep hole in the creek and had just cast my fish hook into the hole.

Suddenly, I heard a noise above me.

I was wearing overalls and a shirt but I had my shirt over the top of my "galluses."

The noise I heard was a snake that had crawled up into the grape vines and it suddenly let go to drop back into the creek.

As it did so it hit the back of my shirt collar and slid down my back—inside my shirt—and out at the tail of my shirt.

I heard it hit the water.

But that wasn't the big thing.

The big thing was that that was the coldest object I ever felt in my life.

And I knew it had to be a snake.

The poisonous snakes we had were copperheads and rattlesnakes. There were no poisonous water snakes in our mountains.

And I figured out quickly that probably the snake I felt was harmless.

Nevertheless, I lost all interest in fishing.

I got out of there. I went home. I never wanted my backbone to be that cold any more.

74

A Solid Foundation—The Rock and the Church

There were two churches located on Lands Creek. Both were Baptist. The lower one was Rock Creek Baptist Church. It puzzled me as a kid that someone would give a church on Lands Creek the name of Rock Creek.

But I had heard that there was a promise in the Bible that upon this rock I will build my church. So I took it that Rock Creek Baptist Church had a solid foundation.

And then one Sunday I learned a different lesson.

Uncle Lige Lowe was the Pastor of Rock Creek Baptist Church. Gram Pa Hyde—although illiterate—was a Deacon. Also a Deacon was the nephew of our Pastor, Mr. Tom Lowe, next door neighbor to Gram Pa Hyde.

One Sunday morning Church was in progress. For some reason I was not inside the church. I was outside, near the dirt road that went by the church. The road was about twenty feet in front of the church.

The Church was one large room with only one door. That door, the only entry, was reached by climbing up a long line of steps.

On that Sunday morning, while I was outside, three young men came up the creek by the dirt road and all stopped in front of the church. It was obvious that all three had been drinking some alcoholic beverage.

That was made even more evident when the three stopped, squatted down in a circle and one placed a half gallon fruit jar full of corn whiskey in the middle of their circle.

They began talking and drinking and—as a short time went on—they became louder.

I was located a few feet away and I simply watched and listened. Then trouble began.

Deacon Tom Lowe came out of the church, approached the three and told them that they were disturbing worship and to move on.

They all stood up. As they did so, one took hold of a large rock with his right hand. He drew back the rock, aiming it at the Deacon. The Deacon broke to run and started up the steps. The rock was thrown with great strength. Just as the Deacon reached the top step, the rock hit the front wall of the Church near his head.

It made a very loud noise.

The three men all laughed and then went walking on up the road.

The next week warrants were taken against the three men for disturbing worship.

When Dad heard about that and also heard that I had been outside and saw and heard all that happened, he decided to attend the trial and to take me with him.

The trial was before a Justice of The Peace. (Both his son and grand son later became lawyers.)

The evidence for the State or prosecution was presented. Defendants offered no evidence.

The Justice of The Peace then declared that it was difficult to determine what amounted to disturbing worship. He said that if someone sang off key while the congregation was singing hymns, people would look at such a person and not give attention to their own singing, that if some woman started nursing her baby, everyone would look at her and not hear the sermon, or if some person got happy and started shouting, everyone would give that person their attention and—he said—Not Guilty.

I was glad Dad took me. I was really beginning to learn.

75

Loud Talk About Secrets

Uncle Guge Weeks, the husband of my Great, Great Aunt Lizie Weeks, had lost his hearing almost entirely.

That, by itself, didn't hurt anyone else but his loud talk to make up for it could.

Prohibition was in effect. It was unlawful to have whiskey. Technically it might have been lawful if the tax on whiskey had been paid but no one did that in the mountains so one could truly say that possessing whiskey was unlawful.

Always on July 4, we went to town to celebrate. And always, as a part of that celebration, men drank corn whiskey.

On one such occasion, Uncle Guge had acquired a jar of corn whiskey, had drunk some of it, and had hidden the bottle close to the railroad track below town at a place called Coal Chute Hill. That is where coal was loaded on the engine to burn and give the engine power.

A crowd of people—over 100—were gathered near Sneed's Grocery Store when Dad and Walt and I walked into town and to that spot.

Uncle Guge saw Dad. And he knew Dad would like a drink of good corn liquor.

Guge shouted out—the whole crowd heard him—and told Dad that he had some good whiskey and described where it was.

Dad grabbed him by the arm and Dad and Guge and Walt and I practically ran to Coal Chute Hill and got the whiskey.

That was the only way to save it.

76

Getting Off That Car All Up and Down Them Tracks

A rthur was a little older than I. He was about Walt's age.
He lived a good distance from town but there was a dirt road all the way to his house.

Sometimes he would walk to town and back on that road. Other times he would walk down to the rail road on the north side of Tuckaseigee River, just below the home of Aunt Lizie Weeks.

The freight train came by there on a regular schedule and the engine usually had as many as twenty box cars attached behind it.

Those cars had - at each end and on both sides—hand rails or metal hooks attached so that the brakeman or other railroad employee could climb up and down them or just climb on and hold on and ride up and down the track as necessary.

Hoboes also used those hand rails to get free rides, either long or short.

Arthur had learned to get a free ride to town.

The freight train usually stopped at the depot in Bryson City.

But on one occasion the freight train didn't stop in town. It kept on running, going east, and at a speed unusual for a train going through town.

I watched it go through town. I was standing near the tracks and I watched until the last car went around a curve and out of sight.

Then I saw someone walking down the track, approaching me. He walked slowly and seemed to be limping.

When the person got closer I saw that it was Arthur. I waited until he stopped near me.

He was all beat up. He was skinned on the hands and on his neck. He was bleeding in spots. His clothes looked torn and dirty.

I knew he had been roughed up in some way.

I asked him what had happened to him. He said he had caught the train in the usual place, expecting it to stop in town but that it didn't stop and he had to get off even if it didn't stop.

I asked him where he got off.

His reply was: "All up and down them dad burn tracks."

77

The Call: To Attention

The pastor of the Spruce Grove Baptist Church was also the pastor of another small Baptist Church where he and his wife were members.

His wife was a fine lady. She set an excellent example for all the girls who were growing up there. She taught them to be ladies by what she did herself.

She wasn't vain. She never showed off. In my opinion she was a good wife for a good pastor.

But all of us are human. And we make mistakes.

That happened to her.

It was March and a beautiful Sunday noon. But the wind was blowing hard—off and on.

Church service had just ended. The pastor's wife had stepped out the front door of the little church house and was standing on the small porch of the church. Most of the church members had gone ahead and were crowded in front of that porch.

She had on a new flowery dress. It draped from the waist and was down to her ankles.

Suddenly there was a great gust of wind and it blew her dress and undergarment over her head. She grabbed down with both hands to place them back in the proper place and she yelled: "Oh, look!"

Everyone looked.

She was highly embarrassed. You could see that.

And just then there came a second strong gust and the scene was repeated.

Again she grabbed down with both hands and yelled: "Well, look agin."

Everyone did.

Then everyone smiled as she dashed down the steps getting off that windy porch.

It was a rare moment in church

78

Cut Off a Tail—And Then

Finally Dad had managed to trade with Will Howell for the Walker fox hound Dad had wanted for so long. And that dog was indeed a Champion. His name was Old Top.

I went fox hunting with Dad and a bunch of his friends for two nights. Both nights that new dog of Dad's led the chase.

Then disaster struck. Old Top got distemper. At least, that is what all the men said who came by and saw him. I didn't know what distemper was.

But in about two weeks he got over it and got back to normal, except for one thing.

His tail was dragging the ground and it appeared that he could not lift it.

Dad's fox-hunting friends said that the distemper had "settled" in his hips and that was what caused that condition.

Again I didn't understand what they meant. But I could see and understand right off that Old Top had lost about all his value so far as those fox hunters were concerned.

One of the most important things about a Walker fox hound is how that dog carries its tail. It is natural for the tail to curl up over the dog's back.

In a Blue Tick or Red Bone or Plott the ears are long and that is important. In a Walker they are short.

Those natural traits must be present to signify a pure bred dog.

Dragging a tail is a sure sign of absolute failure.

I could see very easily that Dad was concerned.

He thought it over for three weeks.

And then he hit on a plan. I don't know how he arrived at it but he asked me to help him carry it out. And, of course, I agreed to do so.

Our barn had a shed attached to the side opposite the corn crib, with the stalls located in between. The shed had a roof but was not walled in and the large locust stakes holding up the outer edge of the roof were placed on top of a large chestnut log, located on the ground.

Dad took Old Top out to the shed. Old Top had a collar around his neck with a chain attached to it. Dad handed me the end of the chain.

Dad had brought his double bitted ax with him. A blacksmith's forge set in the shed and Dad had hot charcoal in it and a soldering iron in the hot coals. The iron was red hot.

Dad cautioned me to hang on to that dog chain for dear life.

He had placed Old Top so that his back was to the chestnut log.

Dad put his double bitted ax in his left hand and then reached and took hold of Old Top's tail with his right hand. Dad pulled the tail back across the chestnut log. Then he poised the ax and struck downward, cutting Old Top's tail off and leaving about four inches as a stump.

Old Top didn't move. I was amazed that he did not do so.

Then Dad laid down the ax and reached and took the soldering iron out of the forge. He took the stump of Old Top's tail in his right hand and applied the soldering iron to the end of the stump.

Then Old Top moved. Again I was amazed, this time by the force Old Top exerted. He let out the longest, loudest howl I had ever heard. And he jumped high in the air, trying to get loose. I held on for dear life as Dad had told me to do. Old Top made two rounds and I held on. He clawed up the inside wall of the shed and I held on. Then he circled and I stumbled over him and fell partly on him. He fell and then jumped up —howling—and lunged again. Dad tried to catch the chain and missed it. Old Top was loose from me, dragging the chain, howling something awful and running at break neck speed up Lands Creek. Dad and I ran after him. He cut off up a branch by the house of Burgin Watkins. We couldn't get near him. We stopped.

Dad said we needed to catch him and take the chain off because he might go away back in the mountains, get the chain hung up on something and starve to death.

But we had to stop. Old Top was almost out of hearing and still howling.

Then he went over a high ridge and we couldn't hear him any more. Sorrowfully Dad said we might as well go back to the house. We did.

We didn't see or hear anything from Old Top for three days. And then I looked up the road and saw him walking home, dragging the chain behind him.

I yelled for Dad. We both ran out to meet Old Top.

And then we were both amazed.

That tail was standing straight up and was healed up at the end of the stump. Old Top was wagging that tail from side to side. And he looked happy. He was glad to see us.

But he was very hungry.

Dad took off the collar and gave Old Top a good, big feeding. He ate. He kept wagging his tail. Then he laid down and went to sleep.

The word got out very quickly. Fox hunters from miles away came to see Old Top and that newly wagging tail. They couldn't believe it. No one could explain what had happened. But it didn't matter. Old Top was once again the most wanted fox hound in that whole country. And again he proved his worth. He kept leading the pack when we went hunting.

I never understood what happened. But what I know is that I was happy.

And I was elated that Old Top was still my friend.

I didn't fall on him on purpose.

But then I figured out that even a dog knows the difference between being stumbled over and being kicked.

79

Taking the Fifth

My brother Carroll was not really mean or cruel. And he wasn't very talkative.

While we were living at the old Jimmy Jenkins place on Lands Creek, Dad planted a field of cane by throwing the seeds out as one would plant a hay field. The cane patch was between the house and the barn so we had a trail cleared out through it. Along the trail stood one of our apple trees.

One day Carroll got upset at our sister Irene and he hid behind that tree. Irene came along the trail and he stepped out and slapped her shoulder.

She was not really hurt but she yelled and ran to the house crying and told Dad what happened.

Dad called Carroll in and asked why in the Dickens did he slap his little sister.

Carroll hung his head, shuffled his feet and answered: "Well, sometimes I jist don't talk much."

I was listening. I didn't condone what he had done. But I did admire him for not lying, not denying and not giving some flimsy excuse.

80

A Plugged Key Hole—
No Greeting

I attended the Lands Creek Elementary School for only a few days. It was located above our new home on Lands Creek about one mile away and just above Spruce Grove Baptist Church and at the intersection of Silver Mine Branch and Lands Creek.

It was a one room, one teacher, seven grade school. The teacher was a fine gentleman who lived west of Bryson City and who drove a car about four miles to Bryson City then about two miles up Bryson Branch where he parked his car. He then walked about two miles across the mountain to the school.

Walt and I had attended school in Bryson City while we lived in Emma Field and after we moved over the hill and lived in a house near the home of Al Ball.

We had both gone to school before that for a short while at Epps Springs which also was a one room, one teacher, seven grade school.

After we moved to Lands Creek I let Dad know pretty quickly that I wanted to go back to town school. That involved about a four mile walk each way except that we could sometimes catch a bus on Bryson Branch. That cut the walking distance down to about two miles and we caught the bus at the point where the Lands Creek school teacher left his car.

Dad told me that I could attend town school if I could put up with the snow and ice and rain and mud and cold weather.

Walt and I said we could and we did.

So, from then until I finished the eleventh grade, I walked out.

Walt finished only the ninth grade and then joined the Civilian Conservation Corps.

There was only one other student who walked out of Lands Creek to the high school in Bryson City. And that was only two years after he had finished the seventh grade on Lands Creek and went through the ninth grade in Bryson City. And, like Walt, he joined the military early in World War II.

After the ninth grade, I was the only student walking out to High School in Bryson City.

All the rest on Lands Creek quit after the seventh grade except Walt and me and that other student. And they stopped after the ninth grade.

So, in my tenth and eleventh grade years, I was the only student to walk out to High School in Bryson City.

In the early years we usually met the Lands Creek school teacher near the gap of the mountain each school day morning as we walked out and he walked in and again in the afternoon as we walked in and he walked out. And, of course, we greeted each other twice a day.

And then one Monday afternoon as we passed he didn't speak to us and he didn't respond to our greetings twice on Tuesday and twice on Wednesday.

On Thursday morning I stopped him and asked him what was wrong. He told me.

When he did, I recalled what had happened on the previous Sunday afternoon.

One of his students in the third grade was named Dave and he had two cousins in the same grade named John and Arthur.

On that Sunday afternoon, Dave chewed up a big mouth full of pine resin (which we called Rausem) and filled the school house one door key hole with it. Next day the teacher couldn't get the door unlocked and it was Tuesday before he got the door open.

When I spoke to the teacher about not greeting me and Walt, he said that I put pine resin in the key hole of the door to the school.

I told him that I didn't do that but that Dave did it.

He responded that Dave told him I did it.

I responded that he should ask Dave's two cousins because they were eye witnesses to what happened.

When we next met the teacher on the trail, he stopped us and apologized. He said that both John and Arthur confirmed what I had told him.

I felt relieved.

After that happened that fine gentleman and I became great friends.

I appreciated the fact that he checked out what I had told him.

81

A Rock Between the Eyes

A bull is a very stubborn animal.
I remember that Gram Pa Medlin's Blue Back Speller said that a bull had a stiff neck and also that the bull bellows and paws the ground.

I learned that from that book and I also learned it from direct observation.

While I was staying part time at Aunt Annie's, I had to walk through a pasture on my way home to Lands Creek.

In that pasture Mr. Franklin had several cows, some horses and one bull. From the stories I heard, confirmed by some evidence I saw, that bull would chase out of the pasture some neighbor women who would go there to pick blackberries. I heard that when the bull started chasing those women, the women would literally run through the barbed wire fence, often leaving rags torn from their clothes hanging on the fence.

I kept out a watchful eye every time I walked through the pasture.

One day, as I walked along the trail through the pasture, I looked and there stood the big bull looking at me.

He twitched his tail. He stuck his nose to the ground. He pawed the earth first with one front foot and then the other. He twitched his tail. Then he bellowed.

I figured it was about time I started protecting myself.

The bull was about thirty feet from me and above me on the hill. I already had a good sized rock in my hand.

I drew back my right hand and I threw the rock toward the bull.

I had a reputation of being a crack shot with a rock.

But I really wasn't as good as it looked later on.

As the rock traveled toward the head of the bull which he held near the ground, he suddenly and swiftly jerked his head upward. I believe his head went up as fast as the rock went down. And, as it did so, the rock hit him in the skull, right between the eyes. The force of the rock and his head lifting was terrific. It knocked him cold.

He fell to the ground. His tongue was out. He lay stiff and still.

I stood there. Amazed.

Then he got up, slowly and staggering. It appeared that he looked at me. Then he turned away and tried to run. He went over the hill at an unsteady pace and he went out of sight.

Always after that when that bull saw me in that pasture, he turned and ran away.

I was grateful.

82

What Some Wine Can Do

While we were regularly attending Rock Creek Baptist Church, I soon found me a favorite time. That was when we took The Lord's Supper.

It was once a year and it came after our fruits and berries had been gathered.

That included grapes. And the drink we had on that occasion was always grape wine, not juice.

The wine was usually furnished by Tom, the nephew of our Pastor, Uncle Lige.

The Church consisted of one room with one door at the back at the top of the steps.

We had no electricity so we furnished lights in the Church with kerosene oil or coal oil lanterns, one on each side of the church on a shelf on the wall and an oil lamp back of the pulpit on a similar shelf.

We usually took the Lord's Supper at Sunday night service.

Perhaps I liked it because I got to drink real wine.

Most of the time the wine would be in a two gallon bucket with a single dipper for drinking. The bucket would start with the Pastor and would pass from row to row. Each person would drink some wine with the dipper.

That fall the time came. Our Pastor called on his nephew to see if he had brought the wine. I was excited, waiting to take part.

His nephew answered that his grapes "didn't hit" that summer and that he didn't have any wine.

We were all let down. There was a collective sigh of disappointment.

And then we heard a voice in the far back from one who usually didn't attend church.

Uncle Fide had come in. He had just moved his family close to the Church and maybe that is why he was there that night.

It was mostly dark in the back but I recognized his voice. So did our Pastor.

Uncle Fide said: "Lige, I've got some wine."

Uncle Lige said: "Well, Fide, go get it." Uncle Fide walked out. He was back in a hurry carrying a two gallon bucket full of his drink with a dipper for drinking.

It started with the Pastor. He drank a dipper full. The bucket went back row by row. I drank a dipper full when it got to me.

What Uncle Fide hadn't told us was that it was persimmon juice, not wine, made from green persimmons at that time of the year. At least that is how it tasted.

A green persimmon is the most stringent fruit I have ever tasted. It has a peculiar ability to draw your mouth almost inside out.

I watched our Pastor. His mouth kept moving to the right and finally, when he spoke, it was under his right ear.

He addressed the flock.

"Well," he said, "I had planned on us singing a hymn but maybe we'd better all just whistle a tune and go home."

83

Surprise or Surprise, Anyhow

I once heard a story about Dr. Samuel Johnson and his distinction between the meanings of the words "surprise" and "amazement." I doubt that Dad's Uncle Fide ever heard that story and, even if he had, it would have made no difference on the one occasion I can think of.

Uncle Fide had finally moved to a house near the head of Noland Creek. That was many, many miles from Bryson City and Uncle Fide didn't make many trips to town. When he did make such a trip he tried to handle all the business he had in one day.

In late fall, Uncle Fide would have a variety of things he could take to town for sale and he could then buy some of the things his family needed. Salt and sugar and coffee were needed. Flour was sometimes purchased by him if he could raise enough cash.

He would take pumpkins for sale, apples, dried beans (leather britches), dried apples, shelled corn, herbs (including ginseng, which we called "sang" and which brought a high price). He may have taken a few gallons of molasses and it is possible he took a few gallons of corn whiskey. He had a mule named Maud and he had a one horse wagon. The wagon had a seat above the bed.

He would fill the bed with his goods, hitch Maud to the wagon and drive to town and there try to find buyers for his goods.

One Saturday he had great sales. He sold all his goods. He felt so good about that after he bought the bare groceries he needed he decided to buy himself a new suit, underwear, shirt, hat and boots. He did so and placed those in the wagon box under the wagon seat.

Apparently he left the wagon for a while, visiting friends. He came back, climbed in and started Maud home.

They reached the last ford in Noland Creek below his house. They were in woods. No one would be in that area.

As he started across the creek, Maud stopped for a drink of water. While waiting for her to finish her drink, Uncle Fide suddenly decided what a surprise it would be for his wife, Bessie, if he came home in his new clothes.

He hadn't had a bath for some time and he decided he could take a bath in the creek and then dress and go on.

Noland is a big, swift creek. Just below that ford the creek went around a curve. It dropped rapidly in elevation.

Uncle Fide removed his clothes and threw them in the creek. The hat was first. It floated out of sight in an instant. It was followed by coat, shirt, pants, boots and underwear. Down the stream went all.

Into the creek went Uncle Fide. The water was cold and swift but he took a good bath.

He climbed on the wagon and opened the wagon box to take out his new clothes and get dressed.

But Lo' And Behold!

Everything was gone.

Someone had stolen all his new clothes and there he stood naked as a jay bird.

He thought a moment and then sat down on the seat and said to his mule: "Aw, heck, Maud, git up and we'll jist go home and surprise Bessie anyhow."

84

The Call to Rock

I was in Bryson City one afternoon in the fall. A close neighbor named Roy came over to me and said he needed my help. He said that he had a pistol in his pocket, that it was against the law for him to carry it, that someone had reported him to the Sheriff's Department and he needed to get rid of the gun right then.

He asked me if I would carry it back to Lands Creek and bring it to the revival meeting at church that night. I agreed to do so and before the service began that night at Spruce Grove Baptist Church, I met Roy and told him I was ready to return the pistol.

He said he couldn't take it then, that two deputies were up the road and that they were watching him. He asked me to keep it and to return it the next day.

I was reluctant because I was going into the church and I was to carry out the second date I had ever had. I was going to walk home a young lady that night who lived in Possum Hollow, about one mile from my house.

I was nervous but I made it through church service and I walked the young lady home, bid her good night and started walking back home. No one had noticed I had a concealed weapon in my front pocket.

The lady I walked home that night had been dating another young man on the creek and had only recently broken up with him.

There was still in that community a practice that was carried on which was cruel, dangerous, unlawful and stupid.

It was called "rocking."

It consisted of a gang of young men getting together above a road or trail after dark, piling up a pile of rocks they could throw, waiting for a young man to come along the road after he had walked some young lady to her home and all in the gang throwing rocks at him as he ran away.

It usually was instigated and organized by some young man who had recently broken up with the young lady the victim had walked home.

I was set up to be rocked.

What I didn't know was that Roy had been requested to be a part of the bunch. He didn't say much to any of them. He simply did not show up when they gathered after Church above the road and waited for me.

The first notice I had of any trouble was when I heard a rock whirring over my head and then saw it land to my left in Lands Creek, making a large splash. Then a second thrown rock hit the middle of the road in front of me.

I was shocked. But I didn't run. I could figure out about where the rocks were coming from. I pulled the pistol from my right front pocket, I cocked the gun. I aimed it up the hill above where I thought the rocks were coming from.

Roy had expected me to do exactly as I did if I did get "rocked."

More rocks were in the air by then.

I pulled the trigger. The pistol fired. I cocked it again. I pulled the trigger again. The pistol fired again.

Then I stopped. I heard a bodacious lot of noise in those bushes up on the hillside where the rocks had been coming from. People were running through the bushes and over bushes, up the hill and over the hill out of hearing.

All was quiet.

I lowered the pistol and went on home.

The next day Roy came to my house and got his pistol.

I told him I had used two shells and offered to pay for them. He wouldn't take any pay.

Roy went on his way.

It was months later that Dad told me he had talked to Roy and Roy told him he knew the rocking was planned and just devised a way to get a weapon to me. He knew the four boys involved in the rocking.

I couldn't feel bad about his effort to help me but he really allowed five young men to go into harm's way without any warning to any of them.

85

Two Blue Feet

Winter set in there on Lands Creek. It was tough. Dad was away working during the winter. Walt was in the CCC's and had been moved over to Brevard. To us that was a long distance.

We didn't have any mule or steer or horse to help pull wood in.

While Walt and I had often taken care of the wood needed by using a cross cut saw, I had no one to help me saw.

We had woods with oak and hickory and beech and birch. There were dead chestnuts scattered around and we could cut those to burn in our cook stove.

But all that wood was a good distance from the house and the only way I could get it to the house was to cut small trees I could pull to the wood yard at the house and cut it into proper lengths with a double bitted axe.

I had been attending school all week and then doing all the chores when I got home. There wasn't much time to get wood. By Friday night we were really low on wood.

On Friday night about eight inches of snow fell.

Early next morning I got the necessary chores done and then I started getting in the wood.

Both of my shoes had a part of the top ripped from the soles. Dad was a fine cobbler and if he had been home, he could have fixed them in a few minutes. But he wasn't home.

I walked through the snow all day. I chopped trees, I dragged them in, I cut firewood and stove wood and I carried it and stacked it on the front porch.

A fire was kept in the fireplace and in the cook stove all day.

Before dark I had a week's supply for both stacked on the porch.

I quit wood cutting and did the other necessary chores. It was dark by the time I finished.

I went inside and I took off my shoes and socks.

I had no feeling in my feet. They were blue. Mom looked at my feet and she told me I had frost bite.

She brought in a wash tub and directed me to place my bare feet in the tub. She poured in enough cold water to cover my feet. I didn't feel the water.

Then she started heating water on the stove and pouring a little heated water at a time into the tub.

Slowly the blue color went out of my feet as she did that and slowly feeling came back into my feet. She did all that slowly, taking over half an hour to finish.

Then I took my feet out and dried them with a towel. They looked normal and they felt normal.

Mom told me that if we had not gone through that procedure, I would have lost all my toe nails and may have suffered permanent injury.

I was mighty glad she knew what she was doing.

86

A Fair Trade

I worked hard during that winter to carry out a project I had dreamed up. I didn't get it finished until spring.

It wasn't a big deal. It was putting together a bicycle.

But I had to cover the countryside to get the right parts: Bryson City, Bryson Branch, Toot Holler, Lands Creek and Buckner Branch.

That last place was across the Tuckaseigee River from where I lived and I remember rowing a boat across the river through floating ice to get there.

Finally I got the thing put together. The bicycle worked well except for one fault. The brakes would not always work and several times as I was riding it down hill and needed to slow down, I would have to run the bicycle up a bank to get it stopped.

A young man close to my age quit school while he was in the eighth grade. He lived between the home of Aunt Annie and my home on Lands Creek.

He observed me on the bicycle on several occasions. He kept wanting to acquire it.

I told him the brakes did not always work but he said that didn't matter. I never told him but my total investment—except for time and work—was only one and a half dollars for the parts.

His name was Albert.

One day he saw me in town and told me that if I would meet him later at Franklin Grove Baptist Church he would swap me a 12 gauge double barreled shotgun, a full box of shells for the gun and one and one half dollars in cash for the bicycle.

I agreed to the trade.

We met as planned and he handed me one and one half dollars, which I put in my pocket, the shot gun and the box of shells. The bicycle was parked, leaning against the bank.

I broke open the shot gun and put two shells in it and then closed it back.

He took the bicycle, straddled it and started coasting downhill toward town.

Suddenly the bicycle fell apart.

We were both shocked.

Neither of us said a word.

He had managed to stand when the bicycle fell apart.

Albert was tall and lanky.

He wrapped his arms around the parts of that bicycle and he turned and headed toward his home, opposite from town. I watched. He disappeared from sight.

Time went by. I just never saw Albert. Finally I finished school, went into the Navy and went through World War II in the Pacific. I returned home and went through college on the G.I. bill. Then I went through law school on a fully paid scholarship.

I was married and my wife and I then had three children. We had moved to Asheville and I was practicing law.

I took a criminal case that had to be tried in Bryson City. One Saturday afternoon I went there looking for a witness I needed to interview.

I searched town for that witness and was told by an acquaintance that probably I could find him in a pool hall just north of the bridge crossing the Tuckasegee River.

I went there and walked in, looking at the players. I walked toward the back and turned, facing the front.

The men's restroom was close by on my right.

Suddenly the door to that room opened and Albert walked out. He stopped and looked at me and blurted out: "Well, I swear. There's the feller that sold me that durn bicycle."

87

Shep Dies

Mom wouldn't agree to let me join the military in World War II before I was eighteen years old. We had had too many relatives killed or wounded.

My Uncle Horace Hyde was killed in the Normandy Invasion.

One of Dad's oldest sister's sons was killed in service. Two of his next older sister's sons were wounded and died at a very early age.

My brother Walt got seventeen battle stars in the Pacific.

I wanted to go.

So I went down to Belmont in Gaston County and got a job the fall after I finished High School. And in December, when I was eighteen, I signed up and volunteered.

The military responded and I went into the Navy.

I had some difficulty. I had had both my eyes wounded while I was a boy. But I didn't have glasses. We couldn't afford that.

So when I got to Great Lakes after volunteering, the medical group gave me a rough time. They told me each eye tested at 20 over 200.

I told them I wanted in the Navy to help my country. And I suggested to them if they merely struck a zero off that bottom figure, my eyesight would be 20/20, perfect eyesight.

They took me in.

And after boot camp I wound up in Military Intelligence.

I learned to be a Radioman. And then I learned to copy Japanese radio messages.

We had broken the Japanese code. And they never caught on that we had done so.

I traveled all over the Pacific Theatre—Hawaii, Johnson Island, New Guinea, Melbourne, Australia, back to New Guinea, Hawaii, Midway, Tinian and Guam.

I had my twentieth birthday on Guam. The war had ended a short time before that.

But it was about then I got a letter from Mom.

Shep had died.

Here I was—twenty years old—and my first and greatest dog had died.

Fighting the enemy was easy.

But the news about Shep was devastating.

I really haven't gotten over that yet.

88

Making Molasses

I returned home from the war in the Pacific in 1946. I spent a few months in college and then several months with my uncle and cousin loading and hauling lumber and stave bolts which were used for making large barrels.

I lived at home with Mom and Dad on the old farm of Gram Pa Hyde.

My brother Walt came back from Navy duty in the Pacific a little while before I got home. He bought the farm of Gram Pa Hyde and Mom and Dad and the children moved in.

Walt was involved in a G.I. Bill training program in farming.

Dad had insisted that a field of cane be planted so that we could make molasses from the cane that fall. When that time came I, too, got fully involved.

Walt had bought one mule but when we finally got into making molasses, he bought two more. Mules were used for pulling the cane mill which ground the juice out of the cane stalks. The juice ran into a tub and we then emptied the tub into the boiler. There was a huge fire under the boiler and it boiled the juice into syrup.

The cane mill had a good sized, long pole attached to the top. A mule was hitched to it and traveled in a circle. That turned the cane mill.

One hand was needed to run the cane mill, Our brother Carroll was given that job. Another hand was needed to tend to the boiler. Walt had that job.

One hand was needed to cut and haul in the wood to keep the fire going under the boiler. That was my job.

And—as it turned out—I was also involved in cutting and hauling in another whole field of cane after we had used up all the cane in the field we had planted on Gram Pa Hyde's old farm.

I really believe that it was because we had done such a good job on the cane we had that Dad decided to buy another whole field of cane.

And, I should have mentioned that a fourth hand was needed: the boss or supervisor of the whole undertaking. That was Dad's job.

So all of us worked six days a week. And each day was from about four o'clock in the morning until after ten o'clock at night.

One of the most intriguing and most unexpected parts of the whole matter was that we had an audience of hundreds of people. Making molasses was about out of business. People had quit the practice.

And, somehow, word got out that we were in it in a big way.

Observers came in from all over the county. As a matter of fact, we had some visitors from Jackson County, Graham County and Macon County.

Most of the observers were of advanced age. And many were on crutches or carried walking sticks to help them move along.

They came to observe. And—it seemed to me—many came to criticize.

All of them had grown up and helped in making molasses. All of them knew the mechanics involved.

And many of them found that we were carrying out the job in a way that did not meet the standards they had known.

They told us so. Some said we were making the molasses too thick. Some said we were making the molasses too thin. Some said we were not getting as much juice out of the stalks as we should have gotten. Others said we were wasting our time and our wood in making the fire too hot under the boiler.

I simply could not understand all the negative talk I heard.

But I noticed that every person who came bought at least one gallon of molasses from Dad.

That could have been because the price was cheap—in my opinion.

The time for the first frost was coming on.

And the first rule in making molasses was that the cane had to be cut before frost came.

We made the deadline—but barely. Dad had gone to Wes Wiggins and bought his big field of cane.

This field was over two miles away, over close to the place I was born. It was a big field.

Dad and I pulled the blades from the cane stalks in that field. He cut off the top of the stalk where the seeds are located. Then Dad cut the stalks off at the ground with a mowing blade while I held the stalks and, as he cut the stalks, I loaded them into a sled.

We cut the last stalks and hauled them to the cane mill by sled on the last day before frost struck that night.

But we met the deadline.

The important point was that it extended our work another three weeks. But we kept at it.

And our audience never got smaller. In fact, it grew larger.

And Dad kept selling the molasses by the gallon.

He was charging only one dollar a gallon. It was going like wildfire.

The criticism was still there. Old men and crippled men kept coming every day. And the sales seemed to pick up every day.

Dad was doing well financially.

But it ended.

I was glad to see the end. I got so I could sleep all night long.

It was one of the greatest experiences I ever had.

And it taught me a lesson.

Whatever criticism you might get from the old and the infirm, as long as they like the product and pay the price, maybe you are doing something right.

89

Why Don't You Just Go Fishing? Literally

That fall after Walt and I returned from the war and before we started making molasses, Walt was getting deep into his G.I. Bill project.

One thing he had decided to do was to replace the old smoke house which Gram Pa Hyde had used for so many years. That old building was made from logs and it was used to smoke hams and to store the smoked meat and other food.

Walt had obtained a machine to make cement blocks and he and I had learned how to use it. We mixed concrete and poured it into the machine. When the cement set, we took out the block and let it dry.

We made scores of blocks. Everything was going well.

Then we started building the walls of the new building which would replace the old smoke house.

For a time that went well, too.

But one factor that had to be watched was that Walt was extremely nervous.

He had won seventeen battle stars in the Pacific, while serving on a cruiser. He was an electrician.

One day after the war was over but while he was still aboard ship, an electric box on the ship which he was working on exploded.

That injured him. In fact, it came near to blinding him completely.

And—most of all—it tore his nerves to shreds.

He came home that way. Most of the time he kept himself under control. But things could happen which set him off.

One such event took place while we were building the new "smoke house." Walt was placing the mortar on the blocks and setting the blocks on the mortar. I was stirring the mortar when necessary and our younger brother Carroll and I were carrying the blocks to Walt for him to lay.

Carroll was then about sixteen years old. He was quiet and unobtrusive.

He carried a block to the wall being built and laid the block on top of the wall. He was on the outside of the wall. Walt was on the inside of the wall and had bent over to get some mortar. He was out of sight. But he had laid his left hand on top of the block wall to hold onto while he bent over. Carroll didn't see him and did not notice his hand. He laid the heavy concrete block on top of Walt's hand.

Walt exploded. He pulled his hand out, bruised and in pain.

He explained to Carroll, in a high, nervous voice: "Why don't you jist go fishing?"

Carroll did not reply. He just turned and walked behind the house. The creek was not far below us.

In a very short while, Carroll appeared on the far side of the house walking toward the creek.

He had a fishing pole over his left shoulder.

He took Walt literally.

He went fishing.

90

Biting a Mule's Ears

Another incident set Walt off that fall. We were all working to get the cane cut and hauled and stacked near the mill.

Walt was working one of the new mules he had bought.

He got close up behind the mule for some reason and the mule decided to kick him. It kicked with both hind feet. But Walt was close to it and the kick didn't injure him; it just pushed him backwards.

The nervous tension took over. Walt started kicking the mule in the side. Then he ran in and pounded the mule in the side with both fists.

Then he went the last step. He ran to the mule's head and started biting the mule's ears.

That was when I had to intervene. I got Walt stopped. I hope the mule appreciated that. At least, the mule never kicked at Walt again.

91

Just to Give the Little Children a Fighting Chance Against the Snakes

What has gone on before now in these pages was mostly what happened to me when I was growing up.

That included the time when I returned home from the war for I was still growing up and trying to learn about life.

Then I reached that age of an adult. I married, finished college, attended law school and started practicing law. My wife and I became parents of six children.

And in the course of all that, we were able to acquire a tract of land on Tessentee Creek in Macon County (my wife's home county, where her mother had grown up).

It was a beautiful mountain place. But the only residence had burned down and the fields had grown up in weeds and briars and bushes.

On it were beautiful streams and flowers and berries of all kinds. We all loved it.

And we had picnic areas and a place for our trailer home.

It had walnut trees and wild strawberry patches. It had blackberries and dew berries and huckleberries and gooseberries. It had apple trees and peach trees and persimmon trees.

It had wildlife of every kind. It had wild deer and foxes and raccoons and o'possums and ground hogs and gray squirrels and flying squirrels and ground squirrels and fish hawks and chicken hawks and owls and pheasants and partridges. It also had dangerous snakes: rattlesnakes and copperheads. Both of those were deadly. One bite and you could be dead.

We knew that.

The children loved to run and play in the fields and woods.

I didn't have any cattle on the place. And we didn't raise any crops. I didn't have time for that.

And so I mowed the place with a bush hog to keep down the weeds and the bushes and to keep the fields clean.

One of our neighbors on Tessentee Creek thought it was strange that I would spend so much time mowing the old fields when I was not raising animals or raising crops or running the place as a farm.

He came up to me and posed the question to me of why I, as a lawyer, would waste my time mowing when I was raising no crops and no animals.

I gave him an answer. That answer was that I was doing all that work just to give the little children a fighting chance against the snakes.